J. R. R. TOLKIEN'S

The Hobbit

dramatized by

PATRICIA GRAY

This dramatization of

"The Hobbit"

is authorized by

PROFESSOR J. R. R. TOLKIEN

THE DRAMATIC PUBLISHING COMPANY

*** NOTICE ***

The amateur and stock acting rights to this work are controlled exclusively by THE DRAMATIC PUBLISHING COMPANY without whose permission in writing no performance of it may be given. Royalty fees are given in our current catalogue and are subject to change without notice. Royalty must be paid every time a play is performed whether or not it is presented for profit and whether or not admission is charged. A play is performed any time it is acted before an audience. All inquiries concerning amateur and stock rights should be addressed to:

DRAMATIC PUBLISHING
P. O. Box 129, Woodstock, Illinois 60098.

Based upon the work "The Hobbit"

Printed in the United States of America

(THE HOBBIT)

ISBN 0-87129-427-3

THE HOBBIT

A Play in Two Acts

For Twenty-six Characters
(fewer with doubling) and Extras

CHARACTERS

BILBO BAGGINS	*a Hobbit*
GANDALF	*a great Wizard*
DWALIN and BALIN KILI and FILI DORI, NORI and ORI OIN and GLOIN BIFUR and BOFUR BOMBUR	*Dwarves*
THORIN	*Leader of the Dwarves*
GROCERY BOY	*a Hobbit lad*
BERT ESSIE TOM	*Trolls*
THE GREAT GOBLIN ATTENDANT GOBLIN	*Goblins*
GOLLUM	*a slimy creature*
THE ELVEN QUEEN TWO ELF GUARDS	*Wood-elves*
SMAUG	*the Dragon*

Other Hobbits, Goblins, Elves, etc. may be added as desired, or the number may be easily reduced.

PLACE: *From Underhill, through the Wilderland, to the Lonely Mountain.*

TIME: *Long ago in the quiet of the world.*

ACT ONE

Scene One

SCENE: The houselights dim. The lights come up in front of the curtain, revealing an imaginary part of the world called Middle Earth. We are in the Shire, Underhill, home of the Hobbits. It is a pleasant morning. The Shire is the picture of rural perfection.)

At L sits a well-appointed little Hobbit by the name of BILBO BAGGINS, Esq. He is sitting on the stoop outside his round green door which has a shiny yellow brass doorknob in the exact middle. At the side is a mailbox with several letters in it. Before him is a turntable or lazy Susan, laid with four complete breakfasts. BILBO has just eaten the first of these and lets out a deep sigh of satisfaction. He carefully dabs his mouth with a huge napkin. Emitting another sigh, he turns the table so that breakfast number two is before him. He digs in with determination after a brief hesitation over which jam to spread his muffin with.)

From R an extraordinary old man /GANDALF/ enters. He is tall, with a flowing white beard and bushy black brows, out of which gleam deep, piercing eyes. On his head is a tall, peaked hat covered with strange designs. He wears a long gray cloak, a silver scarf, and immense black boots, and carries a staff.)

GANDALF (regarding the scene with relish, taking a deep breath of the sparkling air). Ah, the Shire! How delicious the morning is in this part of the world! The air is stuffed with comfort! It feels like nothing exciting has happened here for ages--all green and still---- (Crosses to BILBO, who is well into his third breakfast.) --rather like the inside of one of those fresh eggs you're eating--don't you think?

BILBO (looking up, startled). Oh! I wouldn't know. It's hard to look at a place from the outside when you live in the inside! But then you're a stranger here. Welcome! I still have a breakfast or two left if you'd care for some.

GANDALF. Thank you, I haven't the time--and I am not a stranger anywhere unless, of course, I choose to be.

(A HOBBIT with a green, pointed cap peeks down at them from a window flap in the curtain. Immediately, two more HOBBITS pop out from the two sides of the curtain.)

BILBO (confused). Oh, yes? Well, how do you do, sir---- (Offering his hand).

GANDALF (ignoring the gesture). Magnificently, of course! (Slowly and deliberately.) But at the moment, I am looking for someone to share a great adventure---- (Pauses to see Bilbo's reaction, which is sheer horror.) --a stupendous adventure that I'm arranging--and it's very difficult to find anyone---- (The three HOBBITS who have been listening suddenly vanish. We hear sounds of doors and shutters slamming offstage.) What was that?

BILBO (standing up, taking from his pocket a long wooden pipe and tapping it impatiently). That was neighbors slamming doors and shutters.

GANDALF (sadly). On adventure. Tch, tch.

BILBO. You, sir, are in the neighborhood of Hobbits.

GANDALF (feigning ignorance). Hobbit? Hobbit? What's a Hobbit?

BILBO. We're just plain folk--have no use for adventures. (Shudders.) Nasty, uncomfortable things! Adventures make you late for dinner! Can't think what anybody sees in them! (GANDALF continues to stare at BILBO with a strangely disturbing gleam in his eye. BILBO nervously crosses to the mailbox and removes some letters. He sits on the stoop and examines them.) Good morning, we don't want any adventures here. You might try across The Hill or over The Water. (BILBO devotes himself to his letters.)

GANDALF. You should be ashamed of yourself, Bilbo Baggins!

BILBO (sitting up alertly). That's my name! How did you know----

GANDALF (cutting in). You know mine, too, although you don't know that I belong to it. I am Gandalf, and Gandalf means me! To think that I should have lived to be good-morninged by Belladonna Took's son--as if I were selling buttons at the door!

BILBO (beside himself with excitement). Gandalf! Gandalf! Good gracious! Not the wandering wizard who used to tell such wonderful tales at parties about dragons and giants and goblins----

GANDALF (merely yawning). The same, dear boy.

BILBO. And about the rescue of princesses and the unexpected luck of widows' sons! And the fireworks! I remember those! Old Grandpa Took used to send them up on Midsummer's Eve. What a display!

GANDALF. Naturally.

BILBO. Up they rose, like great lilies and snapdragons, and hung in the twilight all evening, falling at last like silver and gold rain! . . . Dear me! Are you the same Gandalf who led so many of our quiet lads and lasses off on mad adventures? Bless me, life used to be quite inter----I mean, you used to upset things quite badly in these parts! I beg your pardon, but I had no idea you were still in business.

GANDALF. Where else should I be? Tch, tch. Well, for your Grandfather Took's sake and for the sake of your poor mother, Belladonna, I'll give you what you asked for.

BILBO. But I haven't asked for anything!

GANDALF. Yes, you have. My pardon--I give it to you. In fact, I will be so kind as to send you on an adventure--very amusing for me, very good for you--and profitable too, _if_ you live through it.

BILBO. _If I live through it_? _Sorry_. No adventures, thank _you_. _Good morning_! (Starts for his door, then remembers his manners.) I'd ask you in to tea, but----

GANDALF. How kind of you to ask me--I hate to think alone! (Propelling him through the door.) You go along in and fix the tea. I'll be in shortly--I have a little business to attend to. (Gives BILBO a final shove through the door, then chuckles slyly to himself, rubs his hands, and hangs a large, colorful sign on the door. The sign reads BURGLAR WANTS GOOD JOB, PLENTY OF EXCITEMENT AND REASONABLE REWARD. He looks off R.) Ah, here they come! (Goes through door.)

(The curtain opens to reveal the main hall at Bag-End, residence of B. BAGGINS, Esquire. UC is a large round door with a mat in front. To the left of it is a pegged coat-rack. Downstage is a long table, with benches. To the right of the table is a fireplace with a stool before it. GANDALF, at C, looking around the room, calls off to BILBO.)

GANDALF. A fine place you have here, Bilbo.

(BILBO bustles on L with tea trolley.)

BILBO. Yes, I love my quiet home.

GANDALF. I haven't been this way for a long time--not since your grandfather Took passed on----

BILBO. Yes, well, I don't expect there's much to amuse you around here----

GANDALF. True--but you Hobbits make a relaxing change from those dwarves and elves with their hard-headed hustle and light-headed bustle. Do you know the most amazing thing about Hobbits?

BILBO. No, what?

GANDALF. That you remain gentlefolk in spite of everything. I mean I just dropped in and yet you insisted I stay to tea.

BILBO (protesting weakly). Well---- (Doorbell rings. BILBO starts in surprise.)

GANDALF. You expecting someone?

BILBO (crossing to door). No----oh, maybe the groceries.

(BILBO opens the door U C, and in pops a dwarf /DWALIN/ with a blue beard neatly tucked into his golden belt. He wears a dark green hood.)

DWALIN (executing a low, sweeping bow). Dwalin, at your service!

BILBO (baffled, looking for groceries). Why--Bilbo Baggins, at yours! Ummm--I was expecting groceries.

DWALIN. I was told you set a great table.

GANDALF. Ask the fellow in to tea, why don't you?

BILBO. Yes, yes, certainly. Uh, would you care to join us? The kettle's on the boil----

DWALIN. Delighted! (Hangs his hood on a peg and seats himself expansively at table.)
BILBO (sitting down beside DWALIN). Well, now! (Laughs nervously.) Tell me---- (The doorbell rings again.) Oops, excuse me. (Goes to the door, saying while opening it.) I have no idea _who_ it could----Oh!

(There stands an elderly dwarf /BALIN/ with a white beard and scarlet hood.)

BALIN (hobbling inside, gesturing at the coat rack with his cane). Ha! I see they have begun to arrive already! (Hangs his hood next to Dwalin's.) Balin, at your service! (It is difficult for him to execute a bow. He groans.)
BILBO. Thank you. Uh, you said "_They_ have begun to arrive"?
GANDALF (calling). Groceries, Bilbo?
BILBO. Actually, no---- (Taking a deep breath, to BALIN.) Won't you join us for tea?
BALIN. A glass of buttermilk would suit me better, if it's all the same to you, my good sir. But I don't mind some cake--seed cake, if you have any. (Crosses to table.)
BILBO (automatically). Oh, lots! Excuse me. (Hurries off L to get the cake.)
DWALIN. No hurry. (To BALIN.) Fine lodgings here, eh, brother?
BALIN (seating himself). Ummm. These Hobbits have the cream. A big thing this is we're setting out for.

(Doorbell rings, bringing on BILBO from L with platter of cakes.)

DWALIN. But dangerous. Terribly dangerous!
BILBO. Not again!

GANDALF (crossing to BILBO). Allow me to unburden you---- (Takes platter from BILBO and passes platter to others. DWALIN takes two cakes and downs them rapidly and is shortly back for more. BALIN takes one and nibbles at it and puts it down on small table. Later BALIN eats it unnoticed.)

(Bell rings again. BILBO rushes to the door and opens it. There stand two dwarves /KILI and FILI/, look-alikes with blue hoods, silver belts and yellow beards. Each carries a bag of tools and spades.)

KILI. Kili!
FILI. Fili! (Both sweep off their hoods and bow.)
KILI and FILI (together). At your service!
BILBO. Baggins, here---- (Weakly.) At yours . . . uh, and your families!
KILI. Dwalin and Balin here already, I see. Let us join the throng! (KILI and FILI hang up their hoods, cross to table and sit down.)
BILBO (horrified). Throng!
GANDALF. Why, Bilbo, I really am surprised! I didn't think that Hobbits mixed with dwarves.
BILBO. They don't!
GANDALF. No? That's odd, since you have so many dwarf friends.
BILBO (confidentially, to GANDALF). I've never laid eyes on them before! If my neighbors knew, they'd be scandalized! Dwarves here! At Bag-End! (Bell rings, and then there is the lively rat-a-tat of a stick on the door.)
DWALIN. That'll be Dori, Nori, Ori, Oin and Gloin!
BILBO (horrified, crossing to door). Who? (Hurrying to the door as the rat-a-tat continues.) The nerve!

(BILBO opens the door and there stand no less than five dwarves /DORI, NORI, ORI, OIN and GLOIN/, their broad hands stuck in their gold and silver belts. They bow upon introducing themselves.)

DORI (has a blond beard, dark purple hood, and gold belt; doffing his hood). Dori!

NORI (has a blond beard, pale purple hood, and silver belt; doffing his hood). Nori!

ORI (has a brown beard, orange hood, and gold belt; doffing his hood). Ori!

OIN (has an auburn beard, brown hood, and a gold belt; doffing his hood). Oin!

GLOIN (has a gray beard, gray hood, and a silver belt; doffing his hood). Gloin!

BILBO. Oh!

DORI, NORI, ORI, OIN and GLOIN (together). At your service! (They hang up their hoods.)

BILBO. Where do you all come from? (Crossing to GANDALF, frantically.) There's just no end to them! I must be having a nightmare! (GANDALF pinches BILBO.) Ouch!

GANDALF. You're awake. (DWARVES have been whispering among themselves.)

BILBO (coughing importantly to get the Dwarves' attention). Ahem, ahem. Honored Dwarves, I'm sorry but I'm afraid you've mistaken this for a restaurant. This is a private home. (DWARVES laugh politely at what they think is an attempt at humor.)

DORI (slapping BILBO on the back good-naturedly). Oh-ho, jolly good! Bring out the food.

ORI. Hot cocoa for me, please.

DWALIN (from the table). And more cakes! We're fresh out. Please! (Shows empty plate. There is a terrific banging on the door.)

BILBO (fuming). Stop that pounding! What are you

trying to----

(BILBO pulls the door open with a jerk, and in tumble four dwarves, /BIFUR, BOFUR, BOMBUR, and THORIN/, one on top of the other.)

GANDALF (laughing). Careful, careful! It's not like you, Bilbo, to keep friends waiting on the mat, and then open the door like a popgun! (The DWARVES pick themselves up and bow as they announce themselves, except for THORIN, who was at the bottom of the heap, directly under BOMBUR, the fattest of the lot.)

BIFUR (has a very slight chestnut beard and pale yellow hood; he is the youngest of the dwarves). I'm Bifur!

BOFUR (has a gray beard and a dark yellow hood and a silver belt). Bofur!

BIFUR and BOFUR (together). At your service!

BOMBUR (has a light blue beard and a pale green hood. He is the fattest of the dwarves and is a natural clown. He scrambles off THORIN and bows deeply.) Bombur, at your service! (He indicates THORIN, who was at the bottom of the heap and who stands apart brushing himself off indignantly.) Our great leader, Thorin. (THORIN has a black beard and a sky blue hood with a long silver tassel.)

THORIN (snarling at BOMBUR). Sir! (BOMBUR cringes. They all hang up their hoods.)

BILBO (interceding). My fault. I'm terribly sorry.

THORIN (grunting). Don't mention it. (Gazes regally up at the ceiling, looking at row of thirteen hoods.) I see we are all here.

GANDALF. Quite a merry gathering! (Door bell rings.)

THORIN. Who can <u>that</u> be?

BILBO. Well, I certainly wouldn't know!

(BILBO crosses to door, and opens it, and there stands a Hobbit BOY with a box of groceries.)

GROCERY BOY. Your groceries, Mr. Baggins.
BILBO (quickly). Thank you, lad, I'll take them---- (Takes box and attempts to shut door on boy.)
GROCERY BOY (peering over Bilbo's shoulder). Having a party, Mr. Baggins?
BILBO. Humph.
GROCERY BOY. Dwarves! Cheez, Mr. Baggins--hundreds of 'em! Wait till they hear of this down the road. Dwarves! Like locusts! (BILBO shuts the door rudely on the boy.)
BILBO (sadly). Oh, dear!
THORIN (crossing to table with new arrivals). I trust there's food for the late comers.
BILBO (tight as a coil). Well--I may have a little tea left.
GANDALF. Tea? No, no, thank you. A little red wine and some cold chicken and pickles.
THORIN. And for me.
BIFUR. Apple pie--and coffee, if you don't mind.
BOFUR. And mince pie with cheese!
BOMBUR (already seated at the table, drumming on it with zest). Pork pie and salad! (THORIN gives BOMBUR a disgusted look.)
BIFUR. And raspberry jam and muffins.
GANDALF. Put on a few eggs, there's a good fellow.
DORI (from table). Cold tongue!
NORI. A side of ham!
ORI. Cupcakes!
OIN. Assorted cheeses--if you please!
DWALIN. More cakes and ale!
BILBO (dumfounded). More! (Sarcastic.) Oh, certainly, dig in, dig in! (Heading L for the kitchen with box of groceries.) Don't stint

yourselves! (Grumbling to himself as he goes off.) Seem to know as much about the inside of my kitchen as I do! (Calling back.) I could use some help!

THORIN. Bifur! Nori! (BIFUR and NORI go off L to help Bilbo.) Now! Lower the lamp, Balin. (BALIN pulls down the lamp, which hangs over the table. The lights dim.)

DWALIN (rubbing his palms together). Dark for dark business!

BALIN. Hush! Let Thorin speak!

THORIN (at head of table; standing and clearing his throat importantly). Gandalf, dwarves, and Mr. Baggins!

(BILBO, BIFUR and NORI bustle on L, laden with huge platters of food and drink.)

BILBO. Why so dark?

FILI. We like the dark. (FILI notices BILBO is not serving himself and begins to fill a plate for him.)

DWARVES. Shh----

THORIN. We are met together in the house of our friend and fellow conspirator----

BILBO (protesting). No, no!

THORIN. --this wise and brave hobbit----

BILBO (flattered). Dear me!

THORIN. May the hair on his toes never fall out! All praise to his food. (The DWARVES raise their mugs.)

DWARVES (toasting). Hear, hear! (BILBO has slunk over to his stool in front of the fire where he sits clutching his toes protectively. FILI brings him a plate of food, but BILBO shakes his head. His appetite is completely gone. FILI returns to his own place.)

THORIN. We are met to discuss our plans. We

shall start before dawn on a long, hard journey, so dangerous that some may not live through it or they may reach the misty mountain only to be eaten by the dragon ---- (BILBO lets out a piercing shriek, falling off the stool to the floor, where he lies shaking and twitching wildly. The DWARVES spring up and stare at him in dismay.)

GANDALF (producing * a blue light at end of his staff and crossing to BILBO, prodding him with his foot). Come, come. He's an excitable little fellow. He gets these queer fits, but he's fierce as a dragon in a pinch!

BILBO (shrieking). I'm struck by lightning! Struck by lightning! (DWARVES circle BILBO curiously.)

GLOIN (the doubter, snorting). Humph! It's all very well for you to talk . . . but one shriek like that in a moment of danger might wake the dragon and all his kin. They'd eat the lot of us fast as you'd swallow a dozen cupcakes.

THORIN. It did sound more like fright than excitement. In fact, but for the sign on the door, I'd have thought we'd come to the wrong house.

BALIN. Why, he just turned to jelly right before our eyes! He looks more like a grocer than a burglar!

BILBO (raising himself up with all the dignity he can muster). Pardon me, but I couldn't help overhearing your insults. Am I allowed a few words?

THORIN (condescendingly). By all means.

BILBO. First, I don't know what you're talking about. There isn't any sign on my door--unless of course, you're referring to the dents from all your banging!

GANDALF. Of course there's a sign. I put it there myself.

---

* by using camera flash equipment

THORIN. My good sir, the sign says: "Burglar wants good job, plenty of excitement and reasonable reward." Read it yourself. (Opens door and shows sign.)

BILBO. So! I've been deceived!

GANDALF (to THORIN). You asked me to find a fourteenth man for your expedition--and I chose Mr. Baggins here----

BILBO (incensed). Oh, you did, did you? Well, if you think that I----

GANDALF. --but I'm afraid I've made a sad mistake. This can't be the chap! No, no, I was looking for a member of the famous Took family. Imagine! I mistook him for a Took! (Glowers at BILBO.)

BILBO (stung). But I am a Took!

GANDALF. Really? Tch, tch, the blood must have thinned then.

BILBO. Why, my greatuncle, Bull-Roarer Took----

GLOIN (cutting in). Yes, yes, but we're talking about you!

GANDALF (melodramatically). I said to myself, now here is a hobbit with desires beyond his next cup of tea--but alas, he's just an ordinary run-of-the-Shire hobbit. When adventure knocks, he locks his door and hides under the bed.

BILBO (highly insulted, standing up). Really, this is too much!

GANDALF (to DWARVES). Well, dwarves, you can go back to shoveling coal. The hobbit is afraid to go and you certainly can't set out with thirteen! That's too unlucky!

BILBO (with great dignity). Sir, I must tell you that to uphold the honor of the Took family, I would cross mountains and deserts and fight a hundred dragons! I would----

GANDALF (cutting in). Splendid! Mr. Baggins is with us! (Shakes Bilbo's hand.) Now,

Thorin---- (Crosses to THORIN.)

BILBO (mumbling to himself). Now why did I say that? Bilbo, you're a fool! Now you have put your foot in it!

THORIN (to GANDALF). But are you sure he'll do? You, yourself, said that he----

GANDALF (interrupting). If I say he's a burglar, a burglar he is--or will be when the time comes. There's more to him than you guess or he has any idea of himself. You'll live to thank him, and to thank him that you live.

THORIN. Let us hope so! (Turns to others.) Well, now to get on with the plans. It's late. (All walk over to the table and sit with THORIN at the head, BILBO at his right and BOMBUR next to BILBO.)

GANDALF (spreading a large map on the table before THORIN). Let's have some light on this. (BOMBUR adjusts the overhanging lamp. Lights come up. To THORIN.) This is a map of the Lonely Mountain. It was left by your grandfather, King Thrain.

THORIN. Ah, yes?

BILBO. What mountain?

BOMBUR (giving BILBO a friendly nudge). Where the treasure is! And the dragon. (Makes a gruesome face and hisses alarmingly at BILBO.)

THORIN (studying the map). I don't see that this will help much----I remember the mountain well enough and the lands about it---- (Pointing them out.) Mirkwood--the Withered Heath----

BOMBUR. That's where the great dragons breed! (Makes clawlike, threatening gestures and hisses at BILBO, who manages a sickly smile in spite of being terrified.)

THORIN. There's the dragon--marked in red. Well, we're not likely to miss him, are we! (Laughter from company. Bilbo's laughter lingers on. DWARVES look at him curiously.)

BILBO (nervously). Oh ho ho ha! The---- (Stops, embarrassed.) Dragon! I'm not over-fond of dragons, but then I've never actually known any.

GANDALF (dismissing Bilbo's chatter). You will, you will. (To THORIN.) Look here, Thorin. This circle on the map marks the secret entrance in the mountain--here! (Points to spot on map.)

THORIN. Ha! But is it still secret? That's the question!

BALIN. By now the dragon must know these caves from top to bottom.

GANDALF. Not the secret entrance. It's so well hidden it looks exactly like the side of the mountain. And by the way, I've a key that goes with the map. Here it is. (Hands THORIN a key.) Keep it safe!

THORIN. Indeed I will! (Fastens it on a gold chain that hangs about his neck and speaks with great satisfaction.) Well, now, things begin to look more hopeful. A secret entrance! What luck!

BOMBUR (to BILBO). Arrrgh! Hear him roar? It's almost dinner time. The Dragon's hungry for some nice roasted burglar! (BILBO hides his face in his hands and moans. The other DWARVES chuckle and nudge each other.)

THORIN (turning to BILBO with mock politeness). Suppose we ask our burglar expert to give us his ideas and suggestions----

BILBO (confused and shaky). Well, first off I should like some information. I mean, about the dragon and the treasure and how it got there and who it belongs to, and so on----

THORIN (wearily). Oh, very well----

BILBO. And I'd also like to know about risks, out-of-pocket expenses, time required, wages, etc.

BALIN. He wants to know his chances of coming back alive and how much gold he'll get.

THORIN. His chances are as good as ours. The circumstances are briefly these: Long ago when my grandfather was king, the dwarves settled here-- (Points at map.) --under the Lonely Mountain, and they built the merry town of Dale. Those were the happy days! They made beautiful things just for the fun of it. Not to sell, as we do now. When they needed more gold or emeralds or rubies, they just dug them out of the mountain. There was no end to the supply. But that brought the dragon. Good times always bring dragons. History illustrates----

GANDALF (interrupting). Be brief, won't you?

THORIN (insulted). Very well. There was an especially wicked Dragon called Sm-sm-sm-- (Apologetically.) --his name seems to stick in my throat----

GANDALF (helpfully). Smaug!

THORIN. Yes, curse him! He flew from the east and burned the town. Only a few escaped, my father among them.

BILBO (thrilled). And then?

THORIN. The dragon ate all the dwarves and took their treasure. The fiend! (Pounds on the table.) So now we mean to get back what is rightfully ours, and bring our curses home to Sm-sm-sm----

GANDALF (helping). Smaug!

THORIN. Death to all dragons--especially Sm-sm-sm----

DWARVES (banging their mugs and roaring it out). Smaug!

BILBO (weakly). Hear, hear!

DWARVES. Hear what?

BILBO (flustered). Hear what I've got to say!

GANDALF. Go ahead. Say it!

BILBO. I think you ought to go first to the secret entrance and look around--dragons must sleep sometimes. And now I'm off to bed. You have my blessing. Uh--is there anything I can get you before you go?

THORIN. Before we go, I suppose you mean. You're the burglar and getting inside the entrance is your job.

DWARVES (thundering applause). Thorin!

BILBO. But--but, you see, I may have spoken a little hastily just now. It's an inconvenient time to----

GANDALF (dismissing it). It's nearly dawn. Time to clear up and start. (BILBO tries to attract his attention by pulling at his sleeve, but GANDALF ignores him, and he is equally unsuccessful in attracting Thorin's attention. BILBO finally gives up, shaking his head gloomily. The DWARVES jump up and begin to make tall stacks of the plates and glasses. GANDALF and THORIN remain seated, looking over the map.)

BILBO (squeaking with fright). Please be careful! (Spinning around the room.) Please don't trouble! I can take care of everything after you've all gone!

DWARVES (chanting while clearing table).

Chip the glasses, and crack the plates!
Blunt the knives and bend the forks!
That's what Bilbo Baggins hates--
Smash the bottles and burn the corks!

BILBO (shrieking). My best china! Please be careful!

DWARVES (chanting).

Cut the cloth and tread on the fat!
Pour the milk on the pantry floor!
Leave the bones on the bedroom mat!
Splash the wine on every door!

That's what Bilbo Baggins hates!
So, carefully! carefully with the plates!
(The DWARVES exit with the glasses, platters, etc., BILBO whirling around madly. Offstage there is a tremendous clatter as the curtain falls.)

(Lights come up in front of the curtain. The DWARVES are lined up on the apron, sticks with bundles over their shoulders, ready to start. THORIN is at the head.)

THORIN (pacing impatiently). Well, where's the Hobbit? Where's our burglar?

(BILBO runs on L, puffing profusely.)

BIFUR. Here he is! Bravo!
THORIN. Humph!
BILBO (very put out, catching his breath). Oh, my! Oh, my! The way the morning starts decides the day! It's going to be a miserable day! Hunting dragons! At my age! What a fool I am. Everyone expecting me to be ready at the drop of a hat! (Feels his head. No hat.) My hat! My coat, my brolly, my pocket hanky--my purse----
THORIN (cutting in). Stop fussing!
BILBO (searching his pockets). Where's my diary? If the dragon eats me there'll be no record! My friends back home won't know what happened! And I've got no money----
THORIN (disgusted). Get a grip on yourself, Baggins!
DWALIN (grimly). You'll learn to do without small comforts before we reach journey's end.
GLOIN (disgusted, acting it out). Where's his money? Imagine! Our burglar hasn't any money! (Capers about, imitating Bilbo's fluster. The DWARVES laugh derisively.)

BOMBUR (helpful but mocking). I've a spare hood. The lining is fireproof. It'll keep your hair from being burned when Smaug spits fire at you.

BILBO (politely). Thank you, Bombur, much obliged. (Tries it on. It is very large.) I wish it fitted closer, but the fireproof lining is great. Very great.

(GANDALF strides on from L.)

GANDALF. Are we all ready to start? Ah, Bilbo, I believe you forgot these. (Hands BILBO a handkerchief, a pipe and tobacco pouch, a leather bound journal and a hat.)

BILBO (delighted, stowing them away). Oh, thank you! And my diary! How kind of you! (BILBO is puzzled by the hat. He replaces the hood with the hat and looks regretfully at the lining of the hood. Then with decision he replaces the hood on his head, looks uncertainly at the hat and then tosses it off stage.)

DWARVES (approvingly). Bilbo! Long live our Burglar!

GANDALF. And I remembered you, Bombur. (Hands over a string bag of small, hard cakes.)

BOMBUR. Cakes! Thank you! Where did you get them?

GANDALF. From a friend of mine. He lives far from here. You may yet meet him.

BOMBUR (eating one). It tastes of honey.

GANDALF. Yes, my friend keeps bees. (BOMBUR starts to take another.) You'll need these cakes. Don't eat them right away.

BOMBUR (stowing the cakes away). Need them? With all the food we're taking! But, as you say, Gandalf.

THORIN. Our marching song! (THORIN leads the DWARVES off L. They march off heavily, in step, chanting in gloomy tones.)

Far over the misty mountains cold
To dungeons deep and caverns old
We must away, ere break of day,
To seek the pale enchanted gold!

(GANDALF and BILBO follow closely after DWARVES.)

BILBO (to GANDALF). Couldn't they sing something cheery?

GANDALF. Such as----

BILBO (firmly). Such as "Home, Sweet Home." (As they exit, GANDALF puts his arm around BILBO and laughs.)

ACT ONE

Scene Two

SCENE: In the forest several months later. The curtain rises to reveal a nearly bare stage that is divided into three playing areas. At R there is a platform approximately a foot-and-a-half high that extends in from the right side to about one-quarter of the way across the stage. A similar platform extends the same distance from L.)

AT RISE OF CURTAIN: Lights come up on the platform at L. BILBO is discovered sitting on a log at the edge, legs crossed, writing thoughtfully in his journal with a long quill pen. Behind him, the DWARVES, except for Fili and Kili, are sprawled out, resting. The only sound is that of Bombur's heavy snoring. BILBO finishes with a flourish, blows on script, holds it off admiringly and reads aloud:)

BILBO (reading his entry). "Have just stopped to rest and let Fili and Kili water our ponies. Thought for today: Adventures are not all Sunday strolls in May sunshine. " That's really well put. (Lays down book and massages his feet.) Covered with burrs! (Picks at burrs.) And soaked with these nasty May rains. Bother burgling! I wish I was home with the kettle just beginning to sing!

BOFUR (rousing and leaning on an elbow). You'll wish that again before we're out of this mess.

But go on, I like to hear you read about our adventures.

BILBO. Thanks. (Resumes reading.)"At first I thought adventures were much like picnics. We traveled past pretty farms, and the people seemed friendly. But things have changed lately. See thought for today. We've seen no one all day and there's nothing ahead but black, rainy mountains. As soon as Fili and Kili are back, we should move ahead and make an early camp and have some hot supper."

BOMBUR. Sound idea! (Takes out bag of honey cakes and looks at them. He glances about to see if anyone is noticing, and then slips a cake in his mouth.)

BIFUR (rousing). Did someone say supper?

THORIN (rousing). We should be going on. Where are Fili and Kili? (Offstage cries are heard.)

BILBO (jumping up). I hear something.

DORI (rising). It's Fili.

NORI (rising). And Kili.

BIFUR (struggling to his feet). They're shouting for help!

(FILI and KILI enter. They are drenched, breathless, and gasping.)

THORIN. Where are the ponies? What's happened?

KILI. We lost them. (The DWARVES press forward around them excitedly ad libbing questions: "Lost them!" "How could you?" "Did they run away?" etc.)

THORIN (sternly). Silence, dwarves. Kili, what happened?

KILI. We took them down to water like you said. But the stream bed was almost dry and they wandered out into it drinking at some of the little pools. (Pauses, gulping breath.)

THORIN (sternly). Did you stay with them?

KILI (uncomfortably). I did, until they were settled drinking water. Then I--well, I went along the bank looking for mushrooms to eat.

THORIN. You mean you left them!

KILI. But Fili was watching them from the bank and I ran back the minute I heard him shout.

THORIN. What happened, Fili?

FILI. A great wall of water came thundering out of the mountains. I shouted, but it was over the ponies in a moment. They just tumbled over and over like logs and were gone!

THORIN. All of them!

FILI. Yes.

THORIN. And the food bags?

KILI. On the ponies. (THORIN turns away with a gesture of despair.)

BILBO. But then we've nothing to eat.

BIFUR. We've got the honey cakes.

DWALIN. Wise Gandalf. He knew we'd need them!

THORIN. But maybe we'll have greater need of them later. This isn't a real emergency. We're not starving.

BOMBUR. I am.

THORIN. After all, we've got our burglar here. (To BILBO.) It's up to you, burglar. Burgle us some food.

BILBO. Up to me. I like that! Out here in the middle of nowhere! It needs a magician to find food here. Besides, maybe this is the time Gandalf meant us to eat the honey cakes. Why don't you ask him?

BALIN. He's right. Ask Gandalf. (There is a general murmur of agreement from the DWARVES.)

THORIN. You may be right. (Glances around.) Where's Gandalf?

BALIN. Asleep, probably. I'll wake him up.

(Calls.) Gandalf! (No answer. Louder.) Gandalf!

DORI. He's gone!

ORI. Gone! Oh, no!

GLOIN. Smartest thing he ever did!

BALIN. If I was a wizard I'd vanish, too.

THORIN. Yes--well, I'm sure he had his reasons. We'll have to go on without him.

DWARVES (ad libbing groans, etc.). Oh, no!

THORIN (proudly). We dwarves have always stood alone. Our forefathers didn't depend on magic.

GLOIN. And look what happened--a dragon ate them!

BIFUR. Speaking of eating----

THORIN (crossly). Oh, very well! Bombur, share out the cakes. (BOMBUR rapidly passes out the cakes, starting with THORIN. He comes to BILBO last. BILBO takes the cake BOMBUR hands him. He sees the bag is empty.)

BILBO. But there's none left for you! (All the DWARVES turn to look at BOMBUR.)

BOMBUR (embarrassed). Never mind. I had mine.

BILBO. But you didn't. You just passed them out.

BOMBUR. I ate mine before.

BILBO. You mean that time when Gandalf gave them to you? That doesn't count.

BOMBUR (blurting it out miserably). I ate one just before Fili and Kili came back. I'm sorry!

GLOIN (indignant). You broke into our supplies?

BILBO (calmly). They weren't ours, they were Bombur's. Gandalf gave the cakes to him. Besides, we thought we still had our supplies then.

GLOIN. I still think----

BILBO. After all, I'm the only one concerned. You all had your share, and I say Bombur had the right to eat all the cakes if he wanted to. They were his. (Breaks his cake in two.) Take half of this one, Bombur.

BOMBUR. I couldn't....

BILBO (thrusting it in his hand). Then you'll be wasting food as well as the time we're all wasting, for the cake will just crumble away. Come on--together. (BILBO and BOMBUR each pop the half cake in their mouths, smile and clasp hands in a brief handshake.)

BALIN. The burglar's right. We're wasting time. What's your plan, Thorin?

THORIN. Look over there---- (Gestures L. All look off.)

BILBO. Is that where Smaug, the dragon----

THORIN (cutting in). Of course not. But fierce trolls live there. (All shudder.)

BILBO. What are trolls?

THORIN. Huge creatures, too big for us to fight! They eat dwarves--and Hobbits.

BILBO (aghast). But shouldn't we run? Do we go on right up to where they are?

THORIN. We have to. That's the only way. (Encouragingly.) But there's one way to get the better of a troll. They're night creatures. Sunlight kills them. Turns them to stone.

BALIN. I've heard of that. The thing to do is trick them into staying out of their cave until a ray of sunlight hits them.

BILBO (more cheerfully). That shouldn't be so hard.

GLOIN. But the trolls know this will happen. They're hard to fool. Chances are, they've got you frying in a pan while you're still trying to trick them. (BOMBUR has been sneaking up on BILBO from the rear. He grabs him.)

BOMBUR. Got you! I'm a troll. (BILBO lets out a shriek.)

THORIN (sharply). Order. (To BOMBUR.) No more tricks till we're safely out of here! (To BILBO.) Be quiet. Do you want to bring a band of trolls down on us?

BALIN (pointing to platform R). Look, there's a light over there!

(The platform R is now dimly lit with a reddish glow. We can make out three large figures. They are trolls: BERT, TOM, and ESSIE. They are seated on the ground, toasting mutton on long spits of wood and licking the gravy off their fingers. There is a large wine jug.)

THORIN. So there is! Fili, Kili, you look. Your eyes are sharpest. (FILI and KILI strain to see.)

FILI. It looks like----

KILI. It's trolls! Three of them.

DWARVES (ad lib). Trolls! Ugh! Ich! Oh! (The DWARVES huddle together, except THORIN, who stands apart.)

BOMBUR (sniffing the air deliciously). I can smell mutton cooking! (All sniff the air.)

THORIN. It does smell like mutton.

DWARVES (ad lib). Ummm! Sure does! I could do with some mutton! With mint.

BOMBUR. Mutton with garlic. I'm never wrong about that!

OIN. It's a pity it belongs to the trolls.

GLOIN. Yeh. But . . . wait a minute . . . we have a burglar with us!

BILBO (sarcastically). Ah! So you've finally noticed!

GLOIN (rubbing his hands together). Yes, indeed, a burglar! Bilbo, your chance has come at last!

BILBO (warily). It has?

OIN (to THORIN). It's the burglar's turn.

BILBO. It is?

GLOIN. Now you can show your stuff. (Moves closer to BILBO, until they are nose to nose.) Gandalf said that Hobbits were especially clever at quietly sneaking up----

BILBO (incredulously). You can't mean--the trolls? You want me to burgle trolls?

THORIN (nodding). Exactly.

BILBO (desperately). But I--I thought I was only supposed to burgle the dragon!

THORIN. Later, later. Bring back as much mutton as you can carry. We're hungry, remember. If you run into any difficulty, hoot twice like a barn owl, and we'll come.

BILBO (exploding). What! Are you out of your mind?

THORIN (icily). I beg your pardon?

BILBO (indignantly). Hobbits never hoot! But, no matter. No matter. Forward, Bilbo! (He draws himself up to his full height and walks grandly off the platform.)

DWARVES. Careful, now! Don't come back empty-handed! Good luck!

BILBO (crawling stealthily toward the trolls; turning his head toward DWARVES). Hush! Stop the racket! You'll spoil everything. (Muttering to himself, he continues to crawl toward the trolls.) Dwarves!

(Lights dim on platform L and come up on Platform R as BILBO approaches the trolls' campfire.)

BERT (disgusted). Ugh! I'm sick to death o' mutton, Essie! It's coming out me ears! Mutton yesterday, mutton today, and blimey, if it don't look like mutton again tomorrer! (Turns his back to the fire and tosses his mutton over his shoulder in Bilbo's direction.)

TOM. Never a blinking bit o' manflesh or a nice shoulder of dwarf have we had for a long time! (Faces front, also tossing his mutton over his shoulder.)

ESSIE. Aw, git off! Times been up our way when

yer'd have said "Thank yer, Essie," for a nice bit o'fat valley mutton like what this is.

BERT (taking a healthy pull at the jug). Ugh! No more'n a dribble o'drink left! (TOM grabs the jug.) What the 'ell we was a-thinkin' of to come into these parts beats me! (TOM takes a pull at the jug. BERT gives him a jab in the ribs, causing TOM to choke.)

TOM (coughing). We ain't done badly. We've et a village and a half between us since we come.

BERT (whining). Them villages was barely bite-sized. (BILBO has made his way to the fire and is just about to make off with the discarded mutton when ESSIE spots him.)

ESSIE (wheeling around, catching BILBO by the scruff of his neck and holding fast). Blimey, boys, look what I've copped!

BERT (jumping up). 'Ere, wot's it?

TOM (eying BILBO). Lumme if I know. (To BILBO, prodding him in the belly.) What are yer? Man? (BILBO shakes his head wildly.) --dwarf? (BILBO shakes his head again.)

BILBO (stuttering). Ha--ha--ha--Hobbit!

TOM. A hahahahobbit? Can't say I tasted 'em. Can yer cook 'em, Essie?

ESSIE (pinching BILBO like a soup chicken). Yer can try. Won't make above a mouthful, though--not once he's skinned and boned. Now if there was four and twenty of 'em I might make a pie!

BERT. Hey, you! Any more o'your sort a-sneakin' in these here woods, yer nasty little rabbit!

BILBO (correcting him politely). Hobbit, not rabbit. Yes, lots--no--none at all!

BERT (scratching his head). What d'yer mean?

BILBO (collecting his scattered wits). What I say. (To ESSIE.) There's no need to pinch me, madam.

ESSIE. Shut yer mouth! I can always serve you

on toast--minced!

BILBO (pleading). Oh, please don't cook me, kind ma'am and sirs! I'm a good cook myself and cook better than I cook, if you see what I mean. Besides I like it here with you.

BERT (suspiciously). What's 'e say? (Grabs BILBO by the hair.)

BILBO. Ow!

ESSIE (softening). Ah, poor little blighter, let him go.

TOM. Not till 'e says what 'e means by lots and none at all. I don't want me throat slit in me sleep! (Grabs for Bilbo's feet.) I'll hold his toes in the fire till 'e talks!

(GANDALF's head appears from behind a tree. There is a flash of blue fire from his staff, which the trolls do not notice.)

TOM. No! There isn't time. We have to get back to our cave before sun-up.

ESSIE (hanging on). Give him back. He's mine.

TOM. Well, I'm boss.

GANDALF (sticking his head out and calling in a voice mimicking Essie's). Tom, yer a fat fool!

TOM (taken aback). Essie! Watch what you say!

GANDALF (sticking his head out, mimicking TOM). Yer a swag-belly, Essie!

ESSIE (shrieking). What? I'll give you what for! (Kicks TOM in the shins.)

TOM (howling). Oww! (Releases BILBO and hops about. BILBO runs and hides behind a tree.)

BERT (scratching his head; slow on the uptake). You insult the missus, Tom? (Advancing menacingly on TOM.)

TOM (baffled). Wha'? I didn't say nothing----

BERT (putting his fist in Tom's eye). Liar!

TOM (hopping around in pain). Yeow!
GANDALF (mimicking TOM). Big skunk!
ESSIE (coming up behing TOM and hitting him on the head with a dummy club). Take that!
TOM (howling and rubbing his head). Ow! Ow! What did you do that for! (Picks up club and hits BERT on the head.)
BERT (stunned). Gosh! Ouch! (A bird calls, and other birds chime in.)
GANDALF (stepping out from behind tree, holding his staff high with blue fire coming from it; loudly). Dawn take you all, and be stone to you! (The trolls look at one another agape, and turn toward the voice. The twittering of birds rises to a climax of bird calls, and a great shaft of light strikes the trolls.)
TROLLS. Wha'? Huh? Ugh! (Suddenly they freeze into statues.)
GANDALF (walking around the trolls, waving his hand in front of their faces, touching Bert's hair, etc.). Excellent! Museum pieces!
BILBO (capering wildly). They're stone! They've turned to stone!
GANDALF. Where are the dwarves?
BILBO. Waiting for me to return with some food or to hoot like an owl.
GANDALF (hooting). Whoo! Whoo!
THORIN (at platform L, springing up). The signal! To the rescue, dwarves! (They all groan and follow reluctantly. THORIN runs up to BERT with bravado, brandishing his sword.) On guard, Troll! (BERT does not stir; THORIN lunges fiercely.) Aha! (Still no reaction; THORIN, completely baffled, kicks BERT in the knee.) Yeow! (Holds his foot, hopping in pain. BILBO and GANDALF laugh uproariously. THORIN is startled.) Gandalf!
DWARVES (circling the trolls curiously; ad lib).

Stone! Horrid! What a trio! Solid rock! etc.

GANDALF. A fine pickle you left your burglar in, Thorin!

THORIN. And where were you, if I may ask?

GANDALF. I went to look ahead.

THORIN. And what brought you back?

GANDALF. Looking behind----

THORIN. Exactly! But could you be more plain?

GANDALF. I went on to spy out our road. It will soon become much more dangerous. I had not gone very far when I met some Elf friends--they were hurrying along for fear of trolls. I had a feeling I was needed here and I hurried back. So now you know.

THORIN. We thank you! Pack up the food, dwarves----

GANDALF (picking up two swords from the ground). And don't leave these behind! Hmmm, these were not made by the trolls--the workmanship is much too good. The trolls must have stolen these. Why, these are Elvish blades--with the ancient runes engraved on them. The Elves have cleaved many a goblin with these, I'll warrant. (Hands one to THORIN and one to BILBO.)

BILBO. For me? Why, thank you!

THORIN. I will keep this sword in honor. May it soon cleave goblins again!

BILBO. Oh, dear!

GANDALF. A wish that will soon be granted.

BILBO. I didn't wish a thing!

GANDALF. Come, let's head for the Misty Mountains. You must keep to the proper path, or you'll get lost and have to come back. Remember that: stick to the path!

THORIN. We will,Gandalf.

ELVES (offstage, burst of laughter, then singing).

O! Where are you going
With beards all a-wagging?

No knowing, no knowing
What brings Mister Baggins,
And Balin and Dwalin
down into the valley
in June
ha, ha!

THORIN. Elves! Humph!

(FIRST ELF peeks around the curtain L.)

FIRST ELF. Well, well! Just look! Bilbo, the Hobbit, on an adventure with Dwarves! Isn't it delicious!

(SECOND ELF peeks around the curtain R.)

SECOND ELF. Most astonishingly wonderful!

THORIN. Silly fools!

THIRD ELF (off). Mind you don't step on your beard, Thorin! (Burst of laughter from Elves, off.)

GANDALF. Hush, hush, my friends! Valleys have ears, and some elves have over-merry tongues. We must go quietly. There is grave danger ahead. (They all exit as curtain falls.)

CURTAIN

ACT ONE

Scene Three

SCENE: A cave in the Misty Mountains. Lightning-flashes. Sounds of thunder.)

AT RISE OF CURTAIN: Lights come up on platform at stage L. The DWARVES and GANDALF are huddled together, talking in hushed tones. BILBO sits downstage on platform, writing in his diary. He scribbles industriously, then holds book off and reads impressively.)

BILBO (reading his entry). "This is the first chance I've had to write in ages. We've been driven before the storm for twelve days and nights." (There is a distant roll of thunder and more lightning.) "The mountain path is steep and long. We are now resting in a smelly cave." (He again scribbles rapidly.)

THORIN (in a low voice). This is awful!

GLOIN (holding his nose). Phew!

BALIN. At least it's dry!

GANDALF (to THORIN). If you know a better place, take us there!

BILBO (holding his script off and reading again). "We don't dare to talk too loud--there are goblins in these mountains. All this misery for their gold--and my pride--hardly seems worthwhile. The next time anyone calls me a coward, I'll agree with him and stay home. I'd gladly trade my share of the treasure this minute for a steaming bowl of mutton soup!"

GANDALF. Keep your voices down! Thorin, look, your blade glows--that means goblins are nearby. Keep your eyes and ears open. Goblins are swift as weasels in the dark and make no more noise than bats. (They huddle together, peering in all directions; lightning flashes and sounds of thunder.) Are your guards posted?

THORIN (nodding). Four of them, Gloin north, Bofur south, Oin east and Ori west.

(Lights dim on platform L and come up on platform R. Drumbeats are heard off. The GREAT GOBLIN steps out on the platform, followed by an attendant.)

GREAT GOBLIN (bellowing in a stony voice). Who are those miserable persons?

ATTENDANT GOBLIN (bowing and scraping). Dwarves, I believe, O Truly Tremendous One.

GREAT GOBLIN. What are they doing in my domain?

ATTENDANT GOBLIN (shaking). I'll go and ask them, O Truly Tremendous One.

GREAT GOBLIN (with an awful howl of rage). Ask them? (Kicks the ATTENDANT GOBLIN and bats him over the head.) Beat them! Gnash them! Squash them! Smash them! (Gesturing L.) After them!

(The drumbeats increase as many GOBLINS rush on R with bloodcurdling cries. As they reach C, the lights come up on platform L.)

OIN (reporting). Goblins coming.

ORI. I think they're going to rush us!

GOBLINS (chanting and cracking whips).

Swish, smack! Whip, crack!
Clash, crash! Crush, smash!

THORIN (drawing his sword). Ready, my Goblin-cleaver! (He stands on the edge of the platform.) Ready, Dwarves--and Mr. Baggins. (GANDALF, arms folded, stands aloof watching intently. The GOBLINS rush at the DWARVES. THORIN stabs one with his blade. The other DWARVES back up THORIN, and there are hand-to-hand conflicts. BILBO trips up a GOBLIN who is about to stab THORIN from behind. THORIN stabs another. All conflicts must be rehearsed with extra care so that the tempo is very fast. The GOBLINS fall, howling.)

GOBLINS (ad lib). Aie! He's got a Goblin-cleaver! Watch out! Stay back! (The GOBLINS back off in terror.)

GANDALF (to DWARVES and BILBO). Quick. Now's our chance! Everyone follow me! (Runs off L. Others follow, BILBO last. From off.) Quicker, quicker! (GOBLINS run after them, howling and hooting.)

BLACKOUT

(Lights come up very dimly in cave. BILBO is discovered lying on the ground DC.)

BILBO (sitting up, holding his head in pain). Oooh! My head! Where am I! My head--I must have run into a tree! (Groping.) It's so dark in here I can't see a thing. (Calls loudly.) Anyone here?

ECHO (getting progressively fainter). Here--here--here.

BILBO (getting frightened). Who's that?

(Now gleams appear in the darkness. They prove to be always in pairs, of yellow or green or red eyes. They seem to stare awhile and then slowly fade out and disappear and shine out again in another place. Sometimes they shine down from above. Some of them are bulbous.)

BILBO. Now I remember. The goblins!

ECHO. 'Oblins, 'oblins--'oblins--'oblins.

BILBO. And what are those awful eyes watching me for? (Lowers voice.) I was on Dori's back and someone tackled him and he dropped me!

ECHO. 'Opped me--'opped me--'opped me--'opped me.

BILBO (frightened, to the eyes). Keep away from me, eyes! I wonder what happened to the Dwarves? I hope the goblins didn't get them! (Gasps.) My sword! (Holding it up.) It hardly glows. That means the Goblins aren't near and yet they're still around. Ugh! What a nasty smell! Go away, you horrible eyes! (Realizing, stage whisper.) I know where I am. I'm still in the goblin's cave! They smell that way and these may be just the eyes of bats and mice and toads and slimy things like that. (More naturally.) Cheer up, Bilbo. Fear always helps the thing you're afraid of. You're alive and you've been in holes before. You live in one. This is just an ordinary, black, foul, disgusting hole. So blah! (The eyes begin to flicker out, pair by pair, until all are gone. BILBO brightens further.) If this place were aired and decorated it would be nice and cozy. So now I'll just figure out how to get out of here. (BILBO crawls around on his hands and knees toward stage R.) Seems to be a lake over here--no use heading that way. Ouch! Something hurt my knee---- (Picks up small object.) It's a ring! Someone's lost a ring. Well, finders keepers. I'll just stick it in my pocket so I don't lose it myself. (Pockets ring. Lights come up a little.) I can see better now. (Stands and turns toward stage L.)

(An unobtrusive black rubber float is pulled on stage R. On it sits a slimy creature, dressed in black tights or a shiny rubber diving suit, touched up with vaseline to make it glisten, complete with cap, goggles painted a pale watery green. He sits with a leg dangling over each side of the raft, or with knees bent, and holds a short paddle as if rowing.)

GOLLUM (making a swallowing sound as he is pulled on). Gollum! Gollum!

BILBO (whirling around). What's that!

GOLLUM. It's me--Gollum!

BILBO (peering nervously in Gollum's direction). Who's there?

GOLLUM (in full view now). Bless us and splash us, my preciousss! Here's something to eat! (Guttural.) Gollum!

BILBO (brandishing his blade, while shaking and backing off). Stay back!

GOLLUM (swaying his head from side to side as he talks). What's he got in his handses, hmmm?

BILBO (as fiercely as possible). A sword, an Elvish blade! It came out of Gondolin.

GOLLUM (taken aback, hissing). S-s-s-s-s What iss he, my preciousss? Hic! (More politely.) Whom have we the pleasure of meeting?

BILBO (rapidly). I am Mr. Bilbo Baggins, a Hobbit. I've lost the Dwarves and the Wizard and I don't know where I am--but then I don't want to know where I am. The only thing I want to know is how to get out of here!

GOLLUM (hissing). S-s-s-s-s s'pose we sits here

and chats with it a bitsy, my precioussss----
A Bagginsess! (Rubs his stomach.) It likes riddles, p'raps it does, does it? S-s-s-s-s.

BILBO. You mean me?

GOLLUM. Yesssss----

BILBO. Well, I'd love to, but I'm expected somewhere else---- (To himself.) I hope. (To GOLLUM.) So if you'd kindly direct me to the nearest exit----

GOLLUM (cutting in). S-s-s-s-s stop. First a riddle, yesss?

BILBO (resigned). Very well, if you insisssst! After you----

GOLLUM. S-s-s-s-s say,
What has roots as noboby sees,
Is taller than trees,
Up, up it goes,
And yet never grows?

BILBO. Easy! Mountain. Now if you'll kindly----

GOLLUM (cutting in). S-s-s-s-s so does it guess easy? It must have a competition with us, my preciouss. If we wins we eats if--it tastes better if we earns it. If it wins we shows it the way out. Yessss.

BILBO (resigned). Well--all right. Only, how many of them are you? Who's this "Precious" you keep talking to?

GOLLUM. Our Preciousss Self! We has to talk to someone, doesn't we? We are alone here--forever.

BILBO. So, I see. It's a dreadful place.

GOLLUM. We likes it! We generally passes the time feasting on fishesss and gobbling goblins. S-s-s.

BILBO. Goblins! Ick! I didn't think anyone ate them!

GOLLUM. We acquired the taste. Hic! S-s-s-s-s. (Impatient.) Your turn. Riddle! Riddle!

BILBO. Just a minute---- (Thinking hard.) Ah! --

Thirty white horses on a red hill,
First they champ,
Then they stamp,
Then they stand still.

GOLLUM. Easy! Teethes! Teethes! My preciouss, but we has only <u>six</u>. Now! Ssssss.

Voiceless it cries,
Wingless flutters,
Toothless bites,
Mouthless mutters.

BILBO. Half a moment! (Straining.) <u>Wind</u>! Wind, of course!

GOLLUM (disappointed). Sssssss. Your turns!

BILBO. Uh--

A box without hinges, key or lid,
Yet golden treasure inside is hid.

GOLLUM (having great difficulty). S-s-s-s-s. (Whispers.) What iss it? Ssssss. (Takes a fish out of his pocket and wipes his brow with it.)

BILBO. Well--what is it? The answer's not a kettle boiling over, as you seem to think from the noise you are making!

GOLLUM. Give us a chance; let it give us a chance, my preciousss----

BILBO. Well?

GOLLUM (wiping his brow with fish; suddenly). <u>Eggses</u>! Eggses it is! Sssssss--here's a choice one!

Alive without breath,
As cold as death;
Never thirsty, ever drinking,
All in mail, never clinking!

BILBO (stumped). Ahem--ahem--well now. Just a minute----

GOLLUM (starting to emerge from the raft). S-s-s-s-s-s-s.

BILBO (panic-stricken). Wait! I gave you a long

time to guess!

GOLLUM (settling back in raft, hissing with pleasure). Is it nice, my preciousss? Is it juicy? Is it crunchable?

BILBO (stalling for time). Actually, I never gave a thought to how I'd taste cooked until I set out on this horrid adventure. But I'm sure I'd be terribly indigestible. (False laughter.) Ha, ha!

GOLLUM. S-s-s-s-s--the riddle, answer it! It must make haste. We is hungry! (Wipes his brow with the fish.)

BILBO (pointing wildly at the fish). Fish! That's the answer! Fish!

GOLLUM (angry). S-ss-ss--rotten luckses! It's got to ask us a question, my preciouss, yes, yess, just one more, yesss. Ask uss!

BILBO (frantic). Oh, dear! I can't think---- (Grabs for his sword, puts his hand in his pocket. To himself.) What have I got in my pocket?

GOLLUM (taking this for the question). Ssss--not fair! Not fair, my preciouss, to ask us what it's got in its nassty little pocketses!

BILBO (explaining). But I---- (Thinks better of it.) Well, why not? (Boldly.) What have I got in my pocket?

GOLLUM. S-s-s-s-s. It must give us three guesseses, my preciouss, three!

BILBO. Very well! Guess away!

GOLLUM. Handses!

BILBO. Wrong. Guess again!

GOLLUM. S-s-s-s-s--knife!

BILBO. Wrong! Last guess!

GOLLUM (wiggling and squirming, hissing and sputtering, rocking sideways and slapping his feet on the floor). S-s-s-s-s-s.

BILBO (trying to sound bold and cheerful). Come on! I'm waiting! Time's up!

GOLLUM (shrieking). String or nothing!

BILBO (relieved). Both wrong. (Brandishes his sword.)

GOLLUM (eying the sword). S-s-s-s-s-s.

BILBO (shivering). Well? Show me the way out. You promised!

GOLLUM. Did we say so, preciouss? Show the nassty little Baggins the way out, yes, yess. But what's it got in its pocketses, eh? (Starts to get up.) Not string, preciouss, but not nothing. Oh, no! Gollum!

BILBO. Never you mind. A promise is a promise!

GOLLUM. Cross it is. The Baggins is getting cross, preciouss, but it must wait, yes, it must. We can't go up the tunnels so hasty. We must go and get somethings first, yess, things to help us. My birthday present, that's what we wants now--then we'll be quite safe! (He steps out of his raft and waddles UR.) We slips it on and it won't see us, will it, my preciouss. No, it won't see us and its nassty little sword will be useless, yess--Ssssss. (Exits R.)

BILBO (calling). Hurry up!

GOLLUM (off, letting out a horrible shriek). Aaaaaah! Where iss it! Lost! Lost!

BILBO. What's the matter?

GOLLUM (offstage, wailing). Gone--must find it! Lost! Lost!

BILBO. Well, so am I!

(GOLLUM waddles on from R, on his hands and knees, searching wildly.)

GOLLUM. Cursesss! Must find it!

BILBO. You can look for whatever it is later. You never guessed my riddle. You promised!

GOLLUM. Never guessed--never guessed---- (Light dawns.) What has it got in its pocketses?

Tell us! (Advances toward BILBO.)

BILBO. What have you lost?

GOLLUM. We guesses, we guesses, precious, only guesses. He's got it and the Goblinses will catch it and take the present from it. (Makes a lunge at BILBO.) They'll find out what it can do. The Baggins doesn't know what the present can do. It'll just keep it in its pocketses. It's lost itself, the nassty, nosey thing.

BILBO. I better put that ring on or I'll lose it. (Puts his hand into his pocket and slips the ring on his finger and holds it up.) This?

GOLLUM (rushing right past BILBO, wailing). Cursess, the Baggins is gone--my precious. It has my ring! The ring of power!

BILBO (alone on stage). He ran right past--as if he didn't see me--as if I weren't there. . . . Maybe I'm not! The ring! I wonder if it made me invisible? (Inspects himself.) I can still see me.

(GOLLUM rushes on again from L.)

GOLLUM. Give it back like a good Baggins! Where isss it? (Rushes off R.)

BILBO. A magic ring! I've heard of such things in Gandalf's stories--but to find one! What luck!

GOLLUM (offstage, shrieking). Thief!

BILBO. I could stab him with my blade, but that would be wrong when he can't see me.

(GOLLUM waddles on R, worn out and weeping.)

GOLLUM (sitting downstage). It's gone! (Guttural sobs.) Gollum! Gollum! Thief! Thief Baggins! We hates it, we hates it, hates it forever! S-s-s-s-s. (Recovering.) But he doesn't know the way out--he said so. (BILBO nods silently and sits beside him.) But he's tricksy. He doesn't say what he means--like what was in his pocketses--he knows! He knows a way in. He must know a way out! Yesss--he's off to the back door, that's it! (Springs up.) After him! Make haste! (Runs off L.) Gollum! Gollum!

BILBO. I'll follow him to the exit. Then with luck I can slip out the door! (Runs off L after GOLLUM.)

CURTAIN

ACT ONE

Scene Four

IN FRONT OF CURTAIN: Outside the cave entrance. BILBO's head pops out of the center of the curtain. He looks around warily.)

BILBO. Whew! A narrow escape! (Comes D C, looking himself over.) Torn my cloak! Burst my buttons! But I've got spare buttons at home. I wonder where I am? (Looks off.) Good heavens. This must be the other side of the Misty Mountains! I don't see Gandalf and the Dwarves. Maybe the goblins got them. I'd have to go back in there after them . . . I guess---- (Shudders.) But at least I have Gollum's ring---- (Holds finger up.) Why, I must be invisible this very moment! Fancy!

BALIN (calling, from offstage). Mr. Baggins! Mr. Baggins! Where are you?

BILBO (overjoyed). Balin!

(BALIN pops his head around curtain R. BILBO goes to greet him with outstretched arms; of course he is invisible.)

BALIN. He's not here. But I'm sure I heard him call my name!

THORIN (offstage). Are you certain? (BILBO puts his hand to his mouth and doubles up with silent laughter.)

(BALIN walks on R, followed by THORIN, GANDALF and the DWARVES.)

THORIN. Confound the Hobbit! Still lost!

GANDALF. Keep looking. We can't go on without him. I feel responsible for him.

ORI. Pity you didn't pick someone with more sense!

THORIN. He's been more trouble than he's worth. (BILBO draws himself up, offended.)

OIN. Why couldn't he stick with us?

GLOIN (testily). That's right. I refuse to go back into those awful tunnels to look for the little blighter, drat him! (BILBO kicks his leg.) Ouch!

THORIN. What's the matter?

GLOIN. Dunno--felt as if someone kicked my leg!

GANDALF (to GLOIN). Serves you right if someone did. (Angrily, to all.) Now, either you help me look for him or I leave you here to get out of this mess as best you can. Why didn't you stay with him, Dori?

DORI. Good heavens! Can you ask? Goblins fighting and biting--everybody falling over bodies and hitting one another! You shouted "Follow me, everybody!"--I thought everybody had----

THORIN. And here we are, minus a burglar. Drat him! (BILBO steps down in the middle of them and slips off the ring. He is now visible.)

BILBO. And here's the Burglar!

DWARVES (jumping; ad lib). What! Bilbo! Mr. Baggins! Where did you come from?

GANDALF. Bilbo, my boy! What a relief!

THORIN (to BALIN). A fine lookout you are, Balin!

BALIN. Well, it's the first time that even a mouse has crept by me. I take my hood off to you, Mr. Baggins! (He does, and bows.) You're a great burglar. Balin, at your service----

BILBO (bowing). Your servant, Baggins.

DWARVES (ad lib). How'd you escape? What happened? Tell us!

GANDALF. He can tell us on the way. We must leave at once. (DWARVES groan.)

BILBO. But I'm so dreadfully hungry----

FILI. Me, too----

KILI. And me----

BOMBUR. Me most of all!

GANDALF. Forget it. Hundreds of goblins will be out after us as soon as it gets dark. So tighten your belts and let's go. Better no supper than be supper.

DWARVES. Hear, hear!

THORIN. But where are we going? (Takes out his map.)

GANDALF. Through Mirkwood Forest. (Groans from the dwarves.) It is dark and dangerous but it won't be too bad if you can only remember one thing: the path is clearly marked and you must stay on it. Don't let anything tempt you to leave it even for a moment.

THORIN. But aren't you coming with us?

GANDALF. Impossible. I have pressing business in the South.

THORIN. But you can't desert us now!

GANDALF. We may meet again before all is over and then again we may not. That depends on your luck and courage and good sense. But I am sending Mr. Baggins with you, and there's more to him than meets the eye. (BILBO groans.) Cheer up, Bilbo, don't look so glum. Cheer up, Thorin and Company. Think of the treasure at the end!

BILBO. Do we really have to go through Mirkwood! Isn't there some safer way 'round it?

GANDALF. There are no safe ways in this part of the world. You are over the Edge of the Wild now and there's danger everywhere.

THORIN (studying map, irritably). You said some-about a forest path----

GANDALF. Yes. Straight through the forest is your way now. Don't stray off the path. If you do, it's a thousand to one you'll never find it again and never get out of Mirkwood. And then, I suppose, you'll all be eaten by goblins and I shall never see you again!

THORIN (sourly). Very consoling you are, to be sure.

GANDALF. Come now, enough delay. These woods will soon be thick with goblins! (GANDALF exits R. His voice is heard faintly in the distance.) Don't leave the path! (The DWARVES and BILBO trudge glumly off L.)

CURTAIN

ACT TWO

Scene One

SCENE: Mirkwood Forest, weeks later. The stage is dimly lit. On the platform at stage L are huge gnarled tree trunks. Vines trail the forest floor. On a tree a sign is posted reading "MIRKWOOD. Proceed at your own risk," Along the front signs are placed at intervals: "The Path." The DWARVES and BILBO trudge on L in single file, with THORIN at their head.)

THORIN (pausing on the path). There's just no end to this accursed forest. (Shakes his fist.) I hate Mirkwood more than I hate the goblin tunnels.

BALIN. Misery me! It goes on forever!

OIN. And ever!

GLOIN. And ever.

BOFUR. Gandalf said "Cheer up, I'm sending Mr. Baggins with you. He has more about him than you guess. You'll find that out before long." (Turns sharply to BILBO.) Well, Mr. Baggins? It's been long enough----

GLOIN (angrily). What good's a hobbit? Gandalf left us with a hobbit to help us! Hah!

BILBO. That's right, Gloin. Blame it all on me! I wanted to come on this adventure! I begged you to let me come!

THORIN (placatingly). Now, now, this won't do. We must all stick together.

BOMBUR (slapping his own face). Ouch! Mosquitos

biting! Sticky vines wrapping 'round my throat, roots pulling at my feet! I can't go another step. Go on if you must. I'm going to lie down here and sleep--(Sits.)--and dream of food, if I can't get it any other way. (Curls up, yawns sleepily.) The treasure? I'll be too starved to enjoy it---- (Swats at a mosquito. There is a sudden flash of light.)

BIFUR (jumping). What was that?

BALIN. Those flashes of light again! We'd better circle away from them.

BILBO. But if we circle away we'll have to leave the path!

THORIN. So?

BILBO. Gandalf warned us not to.

BALIN. Bilbo's right.

KILI. So he is.

NORI. Gandalf did say we musn't leave the path. But he didn't know all that was going to happen.

BILBO. I think he had a pretty good idea, all the same.

THORIN. We're all hungry.

ORI. And tired.

OIN. I can't go any further.

BILBO. We must go on. Maybe we'll find some berries.

GLOIN. Find berries in the spring--that's a hobbit for you!

DORI. It's time to rest and eat.

BILBO. Let's stick to the path a while longer. (The lights flash again.)

BOMBUR. I can smell meat roasting.

THORIN. Fili and Kili, go and investigate. But be careful.

FILI and KILI. Yes, sir. (FILI and KILI go out R.)

BILBO. They've left the path. Gandalf said----

THORIN. Gandalf should have stayed with us if he expected to run things.

BALIN. But he did say don't leave the path.

THORIN. Well, we haven't left it. Only Fili and Kili have.

BILBO. Curious--it's so quiet--as horribly quiet as it is before something awful happens.

BALIN (looking off R). Fili and Kili are coming back.

(FILI and KILI come on R and rush up to THORIN.)

FILI and KILI (together). It's Elves! They've got food!

OTHERS. Elves! (The following speeches are said in such rapid succession it is as if one person were talking.)

FILI. We crept up----

KILI. To the lights----

FILI. What a sight!

KILI. In a clearing----

FILI. Lots of Elves sitting 'round a fire.

BALIN. What luck!

KILI. Laughing!

FILI. Eating!

KILI. We couldn't bear it. We ran up to beg some food and poof! The lights went out.

FILI. As if by magic!

KILI. Somebody kicked the fire and it went up--(Gestures widely.) --in glittering sparks----

FILI. And they all vanished!

THORIN. Those were wood-elves.

BOMBUR. Friendly elves! And they've got food!

THORIN. No, no, the wood-elves aren't very friendly. They don't like strangers. Mirkwood breeds distrust. (There is another flash of light.)

BILBO. The lights again!

BOMBUR. Let's all go to the feast!

DWARVES (ad lib). Whoopee! Let's go! (They

start to go, leaving the path at an angle.) Come on, Bilbo.

BILBO (standing fast). Wait! A feast will be no good if we don't get back alive from it.

BOMBUR. Well, I'm going. We won't last much longer without food anway.

BILBO. That's true--I guess.

BIFUR. Come on, Bilbo. (BILBO reluctantly follows the others off the path.)

(The ELVEN-QUEEN and several of her attendant LORDS and LADIES enter from L. The QUEEN wears a trimly fitted garment of forest green and a crown of oak leaves and berries. She carries a wand of carved oak. Her attendant LADIES carry bows and arrows.)

ELVEN-QUEEN. Halt! (DWARVES and BILBO freeze in surprise.)

THORIN. By whose authority do you bid us halt?

ELVEN-QUEEN. I am the Elven-Queen. Who are you that trespass on my domain?

THORIN (stage whisper to BILBO). Quick, Bilbo, make yourself invisible. Put on your ring. (BILBO does so, and from then on he is ignored by all.)

ELVEN-QUEEN (imperiously). Speak.

THORIN (stepping forward proudly). I am Thorin Oakenshield, son of Thrain, son of Thror, King under the Mountain!

ELVEN-QUEEN (disdainfully). A dwarf all the same. Why did you and your folk attack my people?

THORIN. We did not attack them, your majesty. We came to beg because we are starving.

ELVEN-QUEEN. What are you doing in Mirkwood?

THORIN. We are looking for food and drink.

ELVEN-QUEEN (impatiently). But why are you here

at all? (THORIN remains silent.) Come now! (THORIN remains silent.) Very well! You shall all go to my dungeons where you shall remain until you tell me the truth--if it takes a thousand years! Seize them! (The Elf GUARDS grab THORIN and surround the others. To the GUARDS.) How many are there?

GUARD. Thirteen, O Queen.

ELVEN-QUEEN. Away with them. (She exits L.)

FIRST GUARD. Step lively, dwarves!

SECOND GUARD. March! (The Elves march the dwarves off L.)

BILBO (taking off his ring and speaking to it.). Well, my friend, thanks to you I'm still free. We should have stayed on the path as Gandalf warned us. And now they'll all be shut up in a stone dungeon. That's a hard thing! Somehow I must get them out! (BILBO runs off L.)

BLACKOUT

(or CURTAIN)

ACT TWO

Scene Two

SCENE: The dungeon of the Elven-Queen's palace. At rise, the DWARVES are discovered behind the bars of a large prison cell in the center section of the stage. They are seated on wooden stools in attitudes of despondency. THORIN occupies a private cell to their right. On the platform at R there are a table and chairs. On the platform L are a pile of straw and four wine barrels. Also in this section, somewhere in the background, are various possessions of the dwarves: bags containing tools /drills and hammers/; jackets, pad and pencil.)

AT RISE OF CURTAIN: BILBO sits against one of the barrels, writing busily in his journal. As lights come up on platform L, BILBO finishes writing and holds up his diary to see better.)

BILBO (reading impressively). "Well, so far I haven't come up with a plan of escape. I might as well be locked up with my friends. Being invisible day after day is driving me mad. This is without a doubt the dreariest, dullest part of this wretched adventure. At least the dwarves are eating well. I have to steal my scraps of food from the kitchen." (Nods approval and scribbles again.)

THORIN (calling softly to BILBO). Psst!

BILBO (ignoring him, reading again, impressively).

"I'm like a burglar that can't get away but must go on miserably burgling the same house day after day!" (Snaps journal shut.)

THORIN (louder). Psst, Mr. Baggins!

BILBO. Shhh---- (Gets up, looks around and crosses cautiously to Thorin's cell.) What is it, Thorin? The guards will be coming any minute with your food.

THORIN. Then put on your ring. Why aren't you wearing it?

BILBO. I don't like to wear it when I don't have to. It makes me feel funny. What did you want?

THORIN. Did you get off the message to Gandalf?

BILBO. I don't know where to send it.

THORIN. Of course. I get more stupid every day.

BILBO. Me, too. It's hard to concentrate when I'm invisible so much. It's as if I'm not all there.

THORIN. At least do _something_. You're a burglar. Steal! (The other dwarves have gathered at the front of their cage and are listening eagerly.)

BILBO. Well, I could steal the keys--that's not so hard.

THORIN (brightening). You could? Wonderful!

DWARVES. Bilbo!

BILBO. But how would we get past the guards? One invisible ring isn't much good among fourteen.

THORIN. We might escape--somehow.

BILBO. But we couldn't possibly get out of the main gate.

THORIN. Why not?

BILBO. Sealed by elf magic.

THORIN (deflated). Oh. (There is the sound of a key turning in a lock.)

BILBO (hushed tones). The guards are coming. Talk up and distract them! I'll see what I can do about the keys.

THORIN (urgently). Put on your ring, you stupid hobbit! (BILBO smites his brow at his forgetfulness, pulls out ring and puts it on.)

(The GUARDS enter from R. The FIRST GUARD has a large ring of keys fastened by a chain to her belt. The SECOND GUARD carries a tray with a bowl of soup and end of a loaf of bread. The FIRST GUARD takes up her stand by the door, guarding it. The SECOND GUARD brings the tray of food to THORIN.)

SECOND GUARD. Food for you, Thorin Oakenshield. Thanks to our gracious Queen. (BILBO, walking on tiptoe, begins to cross very cautiously toward the FIRST GUARD.)

THORIN (taking the tray). I thank the Elven-Queen and hope to return her hospitality when I have recaptured my castle. Its dungeons are deep.

FIRST GUARD. What's that he says?

SECOND GUARD. He threatens our Queen.

FIRST GUARD. That's treason! Write it down! Write down every word he says!

SECOND GUARD. I've nothing to write with.

FIRST GUARD (rushing forward and barely missing colliding with the tiptoeing BILBO, who leaps aside to avoid him). Here, take this. (Gives him a pencil.)

SECOND GUARD. Now, are you ready to answer the questions of our Elven-Queen?

THORIN. I refuse to answer questions under duress.

FIRST GUARD (leaning forward, excitedly). More treason. Write that down! (BILBO is now crouched by the side of the FIRST GUARD, ready to start removing keys from her keyring.)

SECOND GUARD (writing busily on pad). Prisoner defies our Elven-Queen.

THORIN. Now, Bilbo!

FIRST GUARD. What's that he's saying?

SECOND GUARD. Sounded like he said Bilbo. Dwarves are stupid. Let's get out of here. (BILBO has begun removing the key ring. He is very cautious but his hands are shaking and the keys clink. The FIRST GUARD moves uneasily and BILBO freezes. The FIRST GUARD fumbles for her keys. Doesn't find them. She fumbles again. BILBO extends the keys so that she touches them. She is satisfied and returns her attention to SECOND GUARD.)

FIRST GUARD. He hasn't eaten yet and the others haven't had their food.

SECOND GUARD. Let them do without. (To THORIN.) The tray. Let me have it.

THORIN (throwing it at her feet). Gladly.

DWARVES (roaring approval). Thorin!

SECOND GUARD. If it weren't forbidden, I'd make you suffer for that! But wait and see how you like your dinner--_when_ it comes! It'll be _well salted._ I promise _you_ that.

FIRST GUARD. There's a big feast tonight and _we'll_ be eating like kings! (The GUARDS stalk out with a clanking of the door.)

THORIN (excitedly). Did you get the keys?

BILBO. I did. (He unlocks the cage door.)

THORIN. My word! Gandalf spoke true. You're a fine burglar when the time comes! We're all forever in your service! (THORIN steps out and bows as BILBO unlocks the door.)

DWARVES. Bravo! Mr. Baggins--(All bow.)--at your service!

BILBO. Thank you. At yours. (He bows.) But now what? We're still stuck here in the dungeon and if we go out the guards will grab us and put us right back in! (BILBO crosses despondently and sits on one of the barrels.)

DWARVES (ad lib, uneasily). That's true. He's got a point there, all right, etc.

DWALIN (prodding BALIN). Speak to him, Balin.
BALIN. Why me?
DWALIN. You're the oldest.
BALIN. Uh, Thorin----
THORIN (warily). Yes, Balin?
BALIN. We were thinking that--umm, maybe it might be best to tell the Elven-Queen about our quest--the treasure and all that.
DWALIN (putting in). Maybe if she knew, she might even help us. After all, the dragon has stolen elf treasure, too. They took the Elven crown jewels even!
THORIN (outraged). Tell the Queen? And right away she'd ask for a share! Just because you're cowards you want me to ransom you all with my treasure! A share? What's to stop her from taking it all?
GLOIN. Let's not fight about who gets the treasure until we're out of here.
BILBO (suddenly jumping up, excitedly). I've got it! (Taps the wine barrel.) And to think they've been here all the time! (Crosses to THORIN.) I've got a plan! You won't like it, but it's our only chance! (To the others.) Follow me and all keep together. (The DWARVES look at each other blankly.)
BOFUR. We can't see you, Bilbo.
THORIN. Take off your ring.
BILBO (slipping off ring). Sorry.
BIFUR. There he is.
BILBO. Over here! (DWARVES ascend platform L.) Balin, guard the door in case anyone comes.
BALIN. Right. (Crosses and listens at door.) Not a sound. (Takes up watch, his back against door.)
BILBO. Now. (Coming down eagerly to THORIN.) As you know, we can't escape through the gates. But there is another way out.
THORIN. There is?

BILBO. There's a stream under the wine cellar that joins the river further east, and when the wine barrels are empty like these--(Taps one.) --the guards dump them through a trap door just outside here--(Gestures L.)--and they float away.

BIFUR. How do you know?

BILBO. I've watched them. Lots of times. They go bobbing down the river and the current carries them along to Lake-town. (Excitedly.) And where is Lake-town?

THORIN. At the foot of the Lonely Mountain.

BILBO (triumphantly). Our exact destination.

THORIN. Interesting, but it doesn't help us.

BILBO. Can't you see? We hide ourselves in the empty barrels and the elves dump us through the trap-door along with the empties. We simply ride down to Lake-town. (The DWARVES hear this with complete dismay.)

DWARVES (ad lib). No, no. Not me.

THORIN. Bilbo, no! This is madness!

GLOIN. We'd be battered to pieces!

NORI. Or drowned like kittens!

DWALIN. Who'll let us out? We'll starve to death nailed up in those things. (Kicks a barrel scornfully.)

BILBO. No, no! Don't worry! We'll pack the barrels with straw and seal them airtight, and I'll see that everyone gets out.

THORIN. Great! And just how do we breath?

BILBO. Air holes.

BOMBUR. You're not getting <u>me</u> into one of those! I won't fit, thank goodness!

BILBO. Yes, you will, Bombur, We'll shove you in. (DWARVES all turn away, muttering among themselves. BILBO is annoyed and downcast.) Oh, very well! Then go back to your cozy cells. I'll lock you all in again, and you can figure out a better plan for escape.

THORIN (soothingly). Now, Mr. Baggins, be reasonable.

BILBO. But I doubt I can ever get hold of the keys again. (DWARVES groan.)

THORIN. It seems we have no choice. We'll try your plan. It just might work.

BALIN. But there aren't enough barrels.

BILBO. Most of them are piled out there. (Gestures offstage L.)

DWALIN. I still feel the risk is too great----

BILBO (ignoring him). We'll have to act at once. Time's passing.

BALIN (excitedly). I hear them. Hurry!

BILBO. Are they coming?

BALIN. Not yet. They're down the corridor. Hear them singing? (BALIN slightly opens door R.)

ELVES (chanting offstage R).

Roll--roll--roll--roll,
Roll-roll-rolling down the hole!
Heave ho! Splash plump!
Down they go, down they bump!
Down the swift dark stream you go
Back to lands you once did know.

BALIN. They'll be along for our barrels soon.

THORIN. Line up the barrels. Kili and Fili, bore holes. Gloin, make a list and check every dwarf off as he goes in. Bifur, collect straw from our cells to pad the barrels. Bofur, collect jackets and stuff them with straw to leave in the cells.

BOFUR. Whatever for?

THORIN. Make it look as if we're all asleep. They'll finally figure out how we got away but the longer they think we're still here, the better for us.

NORI (approvingly). Pretty smart! (A scene of great activity follows. KILI and FILI pull tools out of their bags and go from barrel to barrel pretending to bore holes in them while BIFUR brings out armfuls of straw and pokes them into the barrels. GLOIN, with pad and pencil, checks off the dwarves as they go into the barrels. OIN has gone off L.)

OIN (speaking from offstage). Fili, Kili, don't forget we've got barrels off here, too.

FILI and KILI. In a minute. We're coming.

BOFUR (busily stuffing jackets with straw). I hate to leave these good jackets behind.

THORIN. Nori, you and Ori start packing dwarves in. Start with Bombur. He'll be the hardest. (NORI and ORI march the protesting BOMBUR to a barrel.)

BOMBUR. Not me! Let someone else go first!

THORIN. Dwalin, Dori, Oin, you're after Bombur. Line up the rest. Into those barrels fast! Kili and Fili, as soon as you finish boring air holes, head up barrels. Close those outside first.

KILI and FILI (putting aside their drills and picking up hammers). But who'll head up our barrels?

BILBO. I'll do it! (There is a frantic scene of dwarves hopping into barrels. Some of this supposedly goes on offstage, to make the process faster. BILBO is everywhere at once. FILI and KILI go out L, and there is a sound of hammering.)

BALIN (warningly). I think they're coming. They just said, "That's the last of that lot."

THORIN. Leave the door. Over here, quick. Into your barrel.

BILBO. Balin, outside. (BALIN goes out L.) You're next, Thorin.

THORIN. The leader should go last.

BILBO. No time to argue. Into the barrel, Thorin! (Calling offstage.) Everybody in out there? Hurry!

KILI. Just heading up Balin.
FILI. We're coming!
THORIN. But who'll be last?

(KILI and FILI enter L and thrust the protesting THORIN into a barrel.)

BILBO. I'll be last. Hurry, Kili and Fili. (They put the barrel head in place. Off stage shouts are heard.) In with you, Kili and Fili.
FILI. But we can't both fit in one barrel.
BILBO. Into it. (BILBO pushes the protesting pair in and closes the barrel. Suddenly he realizes that there is no one to close his.) But what about me? Well, I'll just have to catch a loose barrel and ride on it. (At the very last he suddenly remembers his journal. He dashes back and grabs it.) Now into the river! (Holds his nose firmly.)

(As BILBO seems to leap off into the river, the GUARDS come surging through the door chanting:)

GUARDS. Roll--roll--roll--roll----

BLACKOUT CURTAIN

ACT TWO

Scene Three

IN FRONT OF CURTAIN: Lights come up in front of curtain to reveal DWALIN, BOFUR, BIFUR, DORI, ORI, NORI, OIN, and GLOIN in various stages of exhaustion and saturation. THORIN and BILBO are sitting at C stage, back to back. Behind them are three of the wine barrels (fronts, indicated by cardboard props). They contain Balin, Kili, Fili, and Bombur.)

THORIN (groaning). I've never felt worse than at this moment!

BILBO (nudging THORIN). But are you alive or dead?

THORIN. Achoo!

BILBO. Are you still in prison or are you free? If you want food and if you want to get on with this silly adventure of yours, you'd better slap your arms and legs and try to help me get the others out while there's a chance! (Stands up.)

THORIN. Uh-huh---- (Gets up painfully.) Ooooh! My knees! My elbows! (THORIN goes over to a barrel and removes the lid.) It's Balin! Come on, old friend.

(BALIN's head pops out. He pulls some straws from his draggled beard.)

BALIN (groaning). Ooooh! I'm too old for this sort of thing.

BILBO (removing lid from another barrel). It's

Kili--and Fili!

(Their heads pop out, and then KILI and FILI crawl out of the barrel.)

KILI. Aaaa----

FILI. Choo!

THORIN (removing the lid from the last barrel). This one's packed solid--must be Bombur.

BOMBUR (wailing from inside). Pull me out!

THORIN. I need help over here. (BILBO, BOFUR and BIFUR go over to barrel. They all reach in and pull.) Push, Bombur.

BOMBUR (still inside). Oooooh! Ugh!

(BOMBUR pops out of the barrel.)

BOMBUR. Ah! I hope I never smell the smell of apples again! My barrel was full of it. To smell apples when you can scarcely move and are sick and cold with hunger is torture! I could eat anything in this wide world now for hours on end--but not an apple!

THORIN. Well, that's all of us. It could be worse --and then again, it could be a good deal better.

BILBO. I'm going into Lake-town for food.

BOMBUR. Good thinking!

THORIN. Then, we'll make camp and wait for you here. In the morning we can start for the Lonely Mountain to drive the dragon from his cave. (BILBO slips his ring on his finger and goes off.)

GLOIN. Maybe he's dead by now. (There is a tremendous distant, bellowing roar.)

DWARVES (ad lib). He's alive. That's Smaug. Now our burglar will steal the treasure for us! (Again the dragon roars.)

BLACKOUT

ACT TWO

Scene Four

SCENE: The Lonely Mountain, outside the entrance to the Dragon's cave. The stage is barren except for a few blackened tree stumps. A few broken mining tools may be lying about at stage R. The mountain is indicated by a 3/4 frame drop, with a practical doorway left of C. Left of the door, the remaining quarter of the drop is scrim /gauze/ so that when lights are brought in front and up behind the scrim portion, you can play the scene in the cave. If this is not possible, travelers may be employed to the same purpose. A scrim, of course, lends more magic to the scene. It is almost sunset and the sky is reddening in the west.)

AT RISE OF CURTAIN: BILBO is discovered busily writing in his journal. He is sitting on the stoop before the cave entrance. Dragon smoke belches from under the entrance. The DWARVES glumly pace around the stage, hands behind their backs.)

BILBO (holding script off and reading it). "And so we have come at last to the Lonely Mountain. What a desolate spot! But Thorin remembers when it was green and fair. According to his map, I am now sitting on the very doorstep of the secret entrance to the dragon's cave. But despite our best efforts, the door remains mysteriously sealed." (Resumes writing silently.)

THORIN (stopping before the door, shaking his fist passionately). Come out and get us then! I'd rather face ten thousand of you than stand here doing nothing.

BILBO (reading from journal again). "I don't say so but our predicament may be a blessing in disguise. I'm not looking forward to burgling old Smaug. No, actually, I prefer just sitting----" (Stops writing and hums pleasantly to himself.)

GLOIN. All that treasure in there! Just waiting to be burgled, and _what_ is our burglar doing for us?

THORIN (approaching BILBO). Just what _are_ you doing, Mr. Baggins?

BILBO (who has been humming happily). Hmmm? You said sitting on the doorstep and thinking would be my job, so I'm sitting and thinking. Come join me. This is certainly the warmest spot on the mountain.

THORIN (angry). Mr. Baggins!

BILBO. That certainly is a fine-looking key Gandalf gave you, Thorin.

THORIN. But there's no keyhole! (Flicks at the key about his neck.)

BILBO. Let's have another look at your map.

THORIN. Again! What for?

BILBO. I just thought maybe----

THORIN. Oh, very well. (Pulls out and opens map. BILBO joins him in scanning it. Droning:) The runes tell us to stand by the gray stone--we've been doing _that_, all right! And the setting sun by the last light of Durin's Day will----

THORIN and BILBO (together). --shine upon the keyhole----

BILBO (cheerily). Well, perhaps today is Durin's Day.

BOMBUR. Wake me when something happens.

(Lies down.)

THORIN. Durin's Day! I never heard of it. I've lost track of time altogether . . .

DWALIN. Our beards will grow 'til they hang down the cliff into the valley before anything happens here! (Suddenly a red ray of sunset light falls upon the cave entrance.)

DWARVES. Look! The setting sun shines on the door!

BILBO. This must be the sign!

THORIN. Push! Hard! (The DWARVES push against the door.)

NORI. It won't budge!

BILBO. The keyhole! Look for the keyhole! (Spots it.) Here it is! The key! Quick, Thorin, try your key while the light still shines on the keyhole.

THORIN (removing the key from around his neck and trying it). It fits! It fits! (Turns the key.) The door is unlocked.

DWARVES. Hooray!

THORIN (standing on the stoop and addressing company). And now is the time for our esteemed Mr. Baggins to perform the service for which he was included in our company. Now is the time for him to earn his reward--by being first to enter the secret door.

DWARVES. Hear! Hear! Bilbo first!

BILBO. Well, I don't think I'll refuse. Perhaps I've begun to trust my luck more than I used to.

GLOIN. Well, well, look at our burglar now! Is this the same safe fellow who was lost without his pocket hankie?

THORIN. Mr. Baggins, this is your opportunity.

BILBO. I have no doubt it's an opportunity, but who's coming in with me? (The DWARVES look the other way, embarrassed. They cough self-consciously and shuffle their feet. BILBO stands to one side.) Any volunteers?

THORIN. Now, that isn't quite fair of you, Mr. Baggins. You know we would go with you if it would do any good. But the moment the dragon sees us he will kill us. Since he can't see you, you'll be safe.

BILBO. I'll lend you the ring.

THORIN. But then you'd be seen. No, no, you better wear it. We'll stand by out here.

BILBO. Hmmmm! In that case, stand by the door. (Slips his ring on.)

THORIN. Good luck, Bilbo, my friend! (Reaches for Bilbo's hand but winds up shaking the air; tries again and misses.) Mr. Baggins?

BILBO (clasping Thorin's hand). Here I am, Thorin.

THORIN (laughing and shaking Bilbo's hand). Oh! Good luck!

(The ELVEN-QUEEN, accompanied by two attendants, rushes on from R. She is followed by a number of her ELVES armed with bows and arrows.)

FIRST ATTENDANT. Halt! In the name of the Elven-Queen. (The DWARVES groan as the ELVES surround them.)

ELVEN-QUEEN (stepping forward). So, Thorin Oakenshield, we meet again! Of course I knew I would find you here. Where is the burglar?

THORIN. What burglar?

ELVEN-QUEEN. Don't try to deceive me. He may be invisible but the treasure isn't! Well, now that we are all here, we can discuss matters. How shall we divide the treasure?

THORIN. No elf has a claim to the treasure of my people! I will not parley with armed elves.

ELVEN-QUEEN. But the wealth of the elves is mingled in Smaug's hoard. Let us discuss that.

THORIN. We will give you nothing! Not a single gold coin. We look on you as foes and thieves!

ELVEN-QUEEN. So you claim treasure that is not really yours. Then how are you better than Smaug? Besides, you need my aid.

BILBO (stepping up to the ELVEN-QUEEN and removing his ring). Have you a better plan than ours, Your Majesty?

ELVEN-QUEEN (startled). Ah, the burglar has decided to show himself! But you're not a dwarf--what are you?

BILBO. A hobbit, ma'm. Allow me to introduce myself. Bilbo Baggins, Esquire, companion to Thorin Oakenshield. At your service. (Bows cordially.)

THORIN (furious). Mr. Baggins! Will you please not interfere----

ELVEN-QUEEN. A hobbit? Then maybe you'll listen to reason. Certainly I have a better plan. Dragons have to be slain. Then we should share the treasure. Part of it belongs to us. The dragon stole it from us.

BILBO. Well, slaying dragons is not at all in my line. I was engaged as a burglar. But if part of the treasure belongs to you, I favor giving it to you.

THORIN. I will not share the treasure. I, myself, will slay the dragon.

ELVEN-QUEEN. With what?

THORIN. With this! (Draws his battered sword.)

ELVEN-QUEEN. You ruined that sword when you struck the troll, not knowing he had turned to stone. Behold the sword of the elves. (Claps her hands.)

(Two ELVES enter carrying a gleaming sword on a purple pillow. They stand before the ELVEN-QUEEN.)

ELVEN-QUEEN. This blade was forged to slay Smaug. Agree to give us our rightful share of the treasure and you shall use it.

THORIN. I will not give up so much as one gold piece of the treasure. All of it belongs to me.

BILBO. But, Thorin, if part of it is really hers----

THORIN (thrusting him aside). Silence, traitor!

BALIN. Thorin, we know the crown jewels of the Elves are in the hoard.

THORIN. I no longer call you friend, Balin.

BILBO. It's a bitter thing if our adventure ends this way. I wish Gandalf could help us now!

(GANDALF enters behind BILBO.)

GANDALF (lifting his staff majestically, with the blue light shining). Gandalf is here!

BILBO. Gandalf!

THORIN (sourly). Well, I never expected to see you again. I expect you're coming around for a share, too?

GANDALF. You are not cutting a very splendid figure, Thorin. But things may change yet. Instead of destroying each other you should destroy Smaug together so that Middle Earth can again thrive in peace and plenty. I bring with me certain knowledge that you will need in order to vanquish him. But I will not reveal it unless you and the Elven-Queen agree to join forces. (The ELVEN-QUEEN and THORIN hesitate and then approach one another and clasp hands, at first reluctantly and then with warmth.)

DWARVES. Hurrah for the Wood-elves! (They toss their hats in the air.)

ELVES. Hurrah for the dwarves! (They drum with their arrows on their bows.)

GANDALF. Excellent!

DWARVES (bowing to ELVES). At your service!

ELVES (returning the bows). At yours! (Elvish laughter.)

GANDALF. The dragon cannot be wounded except for one spot! He wears a diamond waistcoat that protects him from danger, but there is a bare spot just over his heart.

THORIN (excited). Then that's the place to strike.

GANDALF. Quite so. You will only have one chance--if any--and you must use the Elven blade and no other.

ELVEN-QUEEN. He shall have it. (Claps her hands. The ATTENDANTS offer THORIN the sword.)

THORIN (taking it). Many thanks, O Elven-Queen. (Brandishes sword.) Blade! I shall not disgrace you! I shall drive you home to your destiny! (Suddenly realizing.) But how?

GANDALF. Quite simple. Bilbo, you will go in first, wearing your ring. Thorin, you follow, but only as far as the inside of the door, and don't move a muscle or Smaug will see you. Once inside, Bilbo must somehow get Smaug to expose his bare patch.

BILBO. How?

GANDALF. You'll find a way.

BILBO. But----

GANDALF (cutting in). And when you do, signal to Thorin, who will fall upon Smaug and slay him. Good luck to you both. (BILBO slips on his ring and is no longer visible to them.)

BILBO. I'm going in now, Thorin.

THORIN (gesturing to BILBO). I follow, Mr. Baggins. (BILBO steps inside the door, followed by THORIN.)

(Lights dim down in front as they come up in the cave behind the scrim. The den is bathed in a golden red light. The walls and ceiling are covered with every kind of treasure: crowns, coats of silver mail, jeweled goblets, shields, etc. SMAUG lies asleep on a vast pile of precious gems. Bubbling noises and vapors emanate from him. BILBO enters from R. He is dazzled by the light and glittering jewels and rubs his eyes. Suddenly he sees SMAUG and jumps.)

SMAUG (stirring, in a thundering voice). Thief! I know you're there. I smell you and I hear your breath. Thought you'd catch me napping, did you? (Vapors and bubbles increase.)

BILBO (summoning up all his courage). Oh, no, O Smaug. I did not come to rob you. I only wished to have a look at you and see if you were truly as great as tales say. I did not believe them----

SMAUG (somewhat flattered). Do you now?

BILBO. Truly, songs and tales fall far short of the reality! You are the greatest of calamities.

SMAUG. Nice manners for a thief and a liar. Come closer so I can eat--I mean, see you.

BILBO. I don't think that would be wise, O Smaug.

SMAUG. Hmmm, you seem familiar with my name, but I don't remember smelling you before. Who are you? Where do you come from?

BILBO (trying to sound formidable). I come from under the hill and over the hills. I am he that walks unseen. I am Barrel-rider and Ringbearer and Luckwearer and I am here to reclaim the rightful treasure of the King under the Mountain.

SMAUG (snorting and belching smoke). The King under the Mountain is dead, and I have eaten his people as a wolf eats sheep. I laid low the warriors of old, when I was young and tender. Now I am old and strong! Thief in the shadows!

BILBO. I am the clue finder, I am he that buries his friends alive and drowns them and draws them alive again from the water. I am Ringwinner and Luckwearer and Barrel-rider!

SMAUG (gloating). My armor is like tenfold shields, my teeth are swords, my claws spears, the shock of my tail is a thunderbolt, my wings are as a hurricane, and my breath is death!

BILBO (in a frightened squeak). I have always understood that dragons are softer underneath, especially in the region of the, er, chest, but that you are guarded by a diamond waistcoat, if those are real diamonds. I hear they are only fakes.

SMAUG (snapping). Your information is false and the jewels are real. Look at them, fool. My waistcoat is made entirely of diamonds which no blade can pierce! (SMAUG rears up and displays the glittering waistcoat. There is a black spot over the heart, bare of diamonds.)

BILBO (calling off). Now, Thorin!

(THORIN rushes on from R and plunges his sword into Smaug's chest. SMAUG thrashes about wildly, emitting bubbling noises and thick smoke, then collapses and lies still.)

BILBO. Well done, Thorin, well done!

THORIN. What a treasure! (He looks at it and removes a magnificent golden coat from the wall.) Mr. Baggins, here is the first payment of your reward! Cast off your old cloak and put on this! It was my grandfather's. (BILBO removes his cloak, and THORIN helps him into the gold coat.)

BILBO. Thank you! My, my, I feel magnificent! But I expect I look rather absurd. How they would laugh back home in the Shire. Still, I wish there was a looking-glass handy!

THORIN (surveying the treasure). Dividing all this will be a long task.

BILBO. I'll miss all that. I must be going home.

THORIN. But yours is a large share. Very large.

Wait for it.

BILBO. How would I get a large share safely back to the Shire and what would I do with it when I got there? The coat is enough for me.

THORIN. At least take this casket of gold coins. No one can question your right to that. Perhaps you may find good use for it on your return. Things change, and not always for the better.

BILBO (accepting the small casket THORIN offers). I thank you, Thorin Oakenshield, and await the day when you rap again on the door of your faithful burglar.

THORIN. And the Queen-- (Glances around, and his eyes light on a richly encrusted robe of state.) This robe is not dwarf treasure. (Takes it up.) And here is the ancient Crown of the Elves! (Picks up a jeweled crown.) Help carry them, Bilbo.

BILBO. Now let us leave this place. (They leave the cave and join the others. Lights come up again in front.)

DWARVES and ELVES (ad lib). Thorin! Mr. Baggins! Hooray!

THORIN. Rejoice, my friends! Smaug is dead!

ALL. Bravo, Thorin. Bravo, Mr. Baggins!

THORIN (to the ELVEN-QUEEN). Madam, your robe. (He puts it over her shoulders. Her ladies adjust it.) Your crown. (Places it on her head.)

DWARVES and ELVES. Hail Queen of the Elves!

ELVEN-QUEEN. I thank you all. You have grown in stature, Thorin Oakenshield. Dwarves, you have a brave and honorable chief.

THORIN. It was your sword that felled the dragon, Great Queen.

ELVEN-QUEEN (smiling). But your hand that wielded it!

GANDALF. Excellent! (Crosses R and slips out

unnoticed.)

ELVEN-QUEEN. I must return to my kingdom. Farewell, and may dwarves and elves ever live in friendship. And you, Bilbo Baggins, I name Elf Friend forever. (All bow as THORIN, holding her hand high, escorts her off R.)

BILBO. I, too, must start the long journey home. Farewell, friends. (Smiles at them.) Remember, a certain burglar will always be listening for the sound of a dwarf staff beating on his door! (He exits R.)

DWARVES (waving and laughing). Good-bye, Mr. Baggins. We shall miss you!

CURTAIN

NOTES ON CHARACTERS AND COSTUMES

BILBO BAGGINS: He is a Hobbit in his middle years, short, compact, with a well-stuffed stomach. His head is covered with thick, curly brown hair, as are his shoeless feet. He is impeccably outfitted in a bright yellow waistcoat and pea green trousers, and wears a pointed cap, as do any hobbit extras used. He is every inch the proper country gentleman delighting in hearty meals and peace and quiet. He loves his quiet home, but something deep inside longs for adventure. Bilbo's Hobbit habits of caution and conservatism make him at times seem cowardly, but actually he is very brave, loyal and resourceful about getting the group of adventurous dwarves out of trouble. They do not realize this until near the end, so they are apt to make fun of him. To call him "The Burglar" is part of the delightful humor of the book from which the play is made. Bilbo is honest—though when he finds the Ring of Power he keeps it, sensing its importance to their quest. The Ring should not be garish. It is a magical ring and its importance lies in its magic, not in its substance. Any plain band ring will serve. For the journey, Bilbo wears a short warm jacket or cloak, and trousers (or shorts or knickers) held up by somewhat gaudy suspenders. He may or may not wear shoes—hobbits seldom wear shoes as they like the feel of the ground on their feet. At the last Bilbo puts on a gold coat (made of gold paper or an ordinary coat sprayed with gold glitter).

GANDALF: He is a great Wizard. No one knows how old he is, nor even the half of his wisdom. He wears a high-peaked blue hat, painted with mysterious signs, and carries a long staff which can emit blue fire at the end. He wears a long gray cloak with a silver scarf wound around his neck, over which his long white beard hangs down below his waist. He wears large black boots. His keen eyes are shaded by bushy eyebrows, which he uses effectively when matters displease him. He can look about him in time as well as space, so he is sometimes impatient with the follies of those about him. Yet in spite of all his wisdom (or is it rather because of his wisdom?) he is understanding and helpful and kind.

THE DWARVES: They are bearded, and all wear the traditional dwarf clothes. Their belts may be painted with gold or silver paint.

DWALIN: He is a dwarf with a blue beard tucked into a golden belt. He wears a dark green hood and costume.

BALIN: He is the eldest dwarf and brother to Dwalin. His white beard is scraggly and he walks with an aged stoop. He wears a scarlet costume with a golden belt.

KILI and FILI: They are look-alikes and should be dressed accordingly. They wear blue hoods, silver belts and have yellow beards. Each carries a bag of tools. They are young and bouncy, and have high, excitable voices.

DORI: He has a blond beard, a dark purple hood, and a gold belt.

NORI: He has a blond beard, a pale purple hood and a silver belt.

ORI: He has a brown beard, an orange hood and a gold belt.

OIN: He has an auburn beard and brown hood and a gold belt.

GLOIN: He has a gray beard and a gray hood and a silver belt. He is the doubter always.

BIFUR: He has a very slight chestnut beard, a pale yellow hood and a silver belt. He is the youngest of the dwarves.

BOFUR: He has a gray beard, a dark yellow hood and a silver belt.

BOMBUR: He is rather fat and a bit of a clown. He

wears a light blue beard, a pale green hood and a silver belt.

THORIN: He is the leader of the dwarves. He is arrogant, stiff-necked and regal. He wears a black beard and a sky-blue hood with a long silver tassel, and a gold belt. Around his neck is a gold-linked chain.

GROCERY BOY: He is a not-too-intelligent hobbit lad.

THE TROLLS: They are hideous, beefy creatures, rough-spoken and dirty. They are dressed in coarse brown rags and wear necklaces of bones and other distasteful tidbits around their necks.

BERT: He is uncouth and lumpish. He wears a rough, dark fuzzy jacket and trousers and workman's shoes. Pale make-up accented with dark accent lines emphasize his uncouth quality.

ESSIE: She is the feminine counterpart of Bert. She wears a long draggled skirt and a gray, much-worn cardigan. Her hair is drawn back in an untidy bun from which straggling wisps escape.

TOM: He is a slightly younger troll. His clothes and make-up are similiar to that of the others.

THE VALLEY ELVES: They are merry folk with high, teasing voices. They are dressed in bright green suits and little pointed caps. They can be male or female.

THE GOBLINS: They are cruel, wicked creatures with over-sized heads, squashed features and large mouths. They are dressed in dark clothing (tights and leotards if desired) and carry chains, whips and clubs. As the scenes are dimly lit, it would be effective if their faces were decorated with day-glow paint. It can be purchased anywhere —just ask the nearest hippie.

THE GREAT GOBLIN: If a head mask is used, the head should be extra large; otherwise a repulsive mask will give the effect. His costume may consist of black close-fitted trousers and a black turtleneck sweater on which strong zig-zags have been painted in white or silver paint. The leader of the goblins is more imposing than the others. He has a great, stony voice, and is easily roused into frenzies of anger and cruelty.

GOBLIN ATTENDANT and SOLDIERS: They may be dressed similarly to the Great Goblin, but perhaps with a design of linked chain painted across their sweaters.

GOLLUM: He is a black, slimy water creature with bulging "pale-green" eyes. He may wear a skin-tight black rubber suit with cap, but not flippers. The suit may be touched here and there with vaseline to give a wet effect and make it glisten. His make-up is greenish and his eyes may be covered with close-fitting goggles painted a watery green, or they may be outlined with white grease paint or ringed in pale green day-glow paint. He is repulsive and frightening in his coldly vicious way.

THE WOOD-ELVES: They are a different breed from the valley elves—good folk, but more distrustful and aggressive. They can be played by either sex. They are dressed in the colors of the forest, greens and browns.

THE ELVEN QUEEN: The queen of the wood-elves is beautiful and regal. She has great dignity and stage presence. In the beginning, she wears a trimly fitted suit of leaves, forest green in color. She also wears a crown of leaves and berries and carries a short scepter of carved oak. In the final scene, she appears as the Great Queen in a glittering court robe and crown.

SMAUG: He is a vast red-gold dragon. He has a huge coiled tail, sharp claws, and a long white belly encrusted with a diamond waistcoat. He may wear a dragon costume or simply a dragon head mask. The body-frame of his costume can be made out of light wood, as in an apple box or a grocery crate. Cardboard is then tacked on and covered with crepe paper or cloth (possibly iridescent plastic cloth) with scales painted boldly on it, which can be sprayed with glitter or sequins. He wears a waistcoat of the same material, which has been sprayed with diamond glitter. It has a black patch on it just above his heart. Smoke can be made to come out of his mouth by placing incense in a little tin dish and placing it in the bottom part of the dragon's cardboard mouth. This makes marvelous smoke. Also, if a second person is used inside the costume, an atomizer filled with ordinary face powder can be used. The eyes can be made of painted plastic cups, and a tongue can be made simply from painted foam rubber.

PRODUCTION NOTES

CAST. As all experienced directors know, parts can be varied at will according to special circumstances. For example, if the stage to be used is small, the number of dwarves, trolls, goblins, etc. can easily be reduced by assigning speeches of characters omitted to those who are retained. Actually, six or seven dwarves will serve as well as thirteen. Also, the play may be presented by an all-boy or all-girl cast. However, if girls play the parts of Gandalf, Bilbo, or Thorin, they should be costumed as males.

GANDALF'S STAFF. The staff may be wired so that he can produce the blue light at the end at will. A piece of blue gelatine over an ordinary flashlight will give effective color.

THE TABLE-CLEARING SCENE. This scene may be enlivened by using inexpensive plastic plates which can be sailed from hand to hand by the dwarves as they chant their song. This scene should be carefully rehearsed to have an unstudied, casual effect.

OTHER LIGHT EFFECTS. Act One, Scene Three calls for lightning effects, also for electrical effects for eyes of different colors that seem to flick on and off in different parts of the stage. The thunder and rain effects are easily supplied by tape recordings.

THE ELVEN SWORDS. These may be cut out of tagboard and painted with bronze paint. A small, flat flashlight securely taped to the sword handle and shaded with a bit of amber gelatine will supply the glow that indicates that Goblins are near.

THE DWARF-GOBLIN BATTLE. This must be rehearsed carefully, with everyone assigned specific opponents and action, so that there is much stage action and excitement. Individual paired teams of opponents may work out and rehearse individually special business of sneaking up on an opponent or rescuing a friend heavily attacked. Pantomimes of pleas for mercy and striking down the enemy are also effective.

THE TREASURE CAVE. This may be as simple or as elaborate as desired. The effect of piles of treasure can be achieved by mounding stuff on any light framework with a lighted bulb below and sheets of amber or gold gelatine above. If it is desired to have some set effects of court jewels, a stunning effect can be achieved by using boxes with cut-out shapes of jewel-set necklaces, tiaras, etc. Gelatine in appropriate colors of emerald, ruby, and sapphire can be pasted over the cut-outs and lighted from behind by Christmas tree lights strung from box to box.

In all scenes where several characters are on stage at once, it is important that actors not immediately involved should be trained to look with simulated interest at any action and never to disturb the attention of the audience by any movement.

PROPERTIES

GENERAL: Bag-End: (Exterior, in front of curtain): A round green door with brass knob in middle, stoop outside door, mailbox with several letters in it. (Interior): Large round door with sign hanging on its outside, door mat, pegged coat rack, long table with benches, fireplace, stool, small table, lamp hanging over long table. Along the Journey: Platforms, log, two elaborate swords, huge gnarled tree trunks, vines, sign reading "MIRKWOOD: PROCEED AT YOUR OWN RISK"; several signs reading, "THE PATH." Dungeon: Bars of cell (including private cell for Thorin), wooden stools, table and chairs on platform R; jackets, pad and pencil, dwarf bags containing drills and hammers, four barrels, pile of straw, on platform L. The Lonely Mountain: Blackened tree stumps, a few broken mining tools, mountain (see description on page 68). Dragon Cave: Helmets, shields, goblets, jeweled weapons, etc. hung on walls, treasure chests with jewelry (costume jewelry) hanging out. Treasure must include golden coat, casket of gold coins, jeweled robe and crown.

BILBO: Turntable or lazy Susan laid with four separate breakfasts (including jam and muffin in breakfast #2 and eggs in breakfast #3); large napkin; long wooden pipe in pocket; tea trolley laden with plates, mugs, glasses, silverware, etc.; platter of cakes; huge platter of food and drink; journal (earlier given him by Gandalf) and quill pen; jeweled sword (after goblin scene); ring.

GANDALF: Staff equipped to show blue light (see Production Notes); large sign which reads "BURGLAR WANTS GOOD JOB, PLENTY OF EXCITEMENT AND REASONABLE REWARD"; large map; key; Bilbo's handkerchief, pipe, tobacco pouch, leather-bound journal and hat; string bag of small hard cakes (ginger snaps will do).

DWARVES: All the dwarves carry bundles on sticks, bags of tools, etc., and in addition: Balin carries a cane, Kili and Fili have spades, Bombur has a spare hood (very large) and later on, the bag of cakes (at least sixteen) given him by Gandalf. Bifur and Nori bring in huge platters of food and drink. In Act One Thorin acquires a sword which is later (in Act Two) to be exchanged for a bent one. Thorin also has a map.

HOBBIT BOY: Box of groceries.

TROLLS: Camp fire (dummy), meat on long spits of wood, hefty wine jug, club (dummy), two swords.

GOBLINS: Whips.

GOLLUM: Rubber float, paddle, rubber fish.

ELVEN QUEEN: Wand.

ELF ATTENDANTS: Bows and arrows, jeweled sword on purple pillow.

FIRST GUARD: Large ring of keys fastened to belt by chain; pencil.

SECOND GUARD: Tray with bowl of soup, spoon and piece of bread; pad of paper.